In Defense of Mohawk Land

Dendi K. Tinumbang

SUNY Series in Ethnicity and Race in American Life
Edited by John Sibley Butler

In Defense of Mohawk Land

Ethnopolitical Conflict in Native North America

Linda Pertusati

STATE UNIVERSITY OF NEW YORK PRESS

Published by
State University of New York Press, Albany

For information, address State University of New York Press,
State University Plaza, Albany, N.Y., 12246

Production by Cathleen Collins
Marketing by Fran Keneston

Library of Congress Cataloging in Publication Data
Pertusati, Linda, 1959–
    In defense of Mohawk land : ethnopolitical conflict in native
North America / Linda Pertusati.
        p.   cm. — (SUNY series in ethnicity and race in American
life)
    Includes bibliographical references and index.
    ISBN 0-7914-3211-4 (alk. paper). — ISBN 0-7914-3212-2 (pbk. :
alk. paper)
    1. Mohawk Indians—Politics and government. 2. Mohawk Indians—
Land tenure. 3. Mohawk Indians—Ethnic identity. 4. Oka (Québec)—
Politics and government. 5. Oka (Québec)—Ethnic relations.
I. Title II. Series.
E99.M8P46 1997
971.4'004975—dc20
                                                96-15322
                                                CIP

10 9 8 7 6 5 4 3 2 1

For the people of the Mohawk nation,
past, present, and future,
in the hope that they may never forget
and
For all the men, women and children
who struggle for First Nations' rights

Contents

Preface

Many ethno-political conflicts have been directed against the state in order to regain sovereignty over territory lost as a result of conquest and colonialization, as in the case of Northern Ireland and indigenous peoples in Canada and the United States; to establish an autonomous territory, such as the Basques in Spain, the Kurds in Turkey, and the Quebecois in Canada; or, to expand existing territorial boundaries, like the Palestinians in Israel.

In the last twenty years, ethno-political confrontation between aboriginal peoples and the state has been frequently identified as a struggle over aboriginal rights to land and resources. Other important issues such as self-government, economic self-determination, and treaty rights become subsumed under that primary struggle, thus, cannot be addressed without resolving the more fundamental issue of access to and control over a territorial and resource base. Maintaining and regaining a land base is paramount to the survival of aboriginal peoples as nations. For aboriginal peoples, the concept of land is sacred, rooted in a history and a sense of responsibility to that history. Further, land is part of their cultural, social, and religious fabric—it is what constitutes their identity as aboriginal peoples.

In 1990, a small aboriginal territory known as Kanehsatake (Oka), the ancient territorial land indigenous to the Mohawk nation, located in Quebec, Canada, emerged onto center stage of the world community. Similar to other aboriginal nations' struggles, ancient, national, Mohawk resources (land) were once more being targeted by the Canadian state for appropriation for the purpose of economic development. The 1990 Mohawk-Oka conflict is not a new phenomenon, but in fact is simply another chapter in the history of the Mohawk nation's struggle for national liberation against state repression. As a colonized nation, the Mohawk nation serves as an example of a nation forced to engage in armed resistance in self-defense (as a final tactic) to prevent additional state seizure of Mohawk lands.

This conflict serves as an example in which participants acted upon deeply held beliefs, while assigning symbolic (as well as particular) meaning to protest activity. The involvement of the Mohawk Warrior Movement in the 1990 Mohawk-Oka conflict was most visibly expressed by a unified belief in Mohawk national self-determination, or Mohawk nationalism. Here, movement leaders used a language of liberation to describe their own and their constituents' grievances against state repression. Specifically, movement leaders were able to nurture and capitalize on an ideological interpretive frame, "nationalism," to assign meaning to movement participation and protest activity.

In studying how the Mohawk Warrior Movement evolved, one uncovers the processes by which cultural values and beliefs can become a resource for social movements. In this book, I argue that interpretive frames, in this case, politicized ethnicity and ideology, can play an integral role in social movement activities by articulating and elaborating movement goals and strategies.

A few words about terminology are warranted. Churchill (1994) and Deloria and Lytle (1984) argue that the use of the word "tribe" to refer to Native American collectivities is an externally-constructed, inappropriate, and innacurate designation which was and continues to be imposed on indigenous peoples by Europeans and now Euro-americans. Specifically, Churchill (1994) argues that the distinction between American Indians being identified as members of peoples understood to constitute nations in our own right, and being cast as members of groups commonly perceived as comprising something less—a community, say . . . or a tribe—incurs a decisive meaning . . . designed to distort and confuse rather than to inform or clarify discussion of indigenous rights. (p. 293–4)

Throughout this book, the term *nation* is used when referring to the Mohawk. Nation can best be defined as "a politically conscious group that is bounded socially and spatially, claiming statehood rights on the basis of common ethnicity" (van den Berghe, 1983:222). In other words, it implies a sovereign people with the right to economic self-determination and self-government. The term *the state* is best defined as "the power or authority represented by a body of people politically organized under one government within a territory having definite boundaries" (*Webster's New World Dictionary*, 1986:1,390). There are various types of state structures: authoritarian, capitalist, democratic, and socialist, among others. For the purpose of analyzing the ethno-political conflict between the Mohawk nation and the state (the 1990 Mohawk-Oka conflict), this book is concerned with the capitalist state structure of Canada.

In Canada, the term *First Nations* is preferred by some, while others prefer "aboriginal peoples" or "native peoples." In the United States, the term *Native American* is widely used but not preferred by everyone. For the purposes of this book, then, the terms *First Nations*, *aboriginal peoples*, and *indigenous peoples*, will be used interchangeably, to denote an all-embracing identification for those peoples who are descendents of the original inhabitants of what is now known as Canada and the United States. "Nationalism," then, is an ideology that can be a foundation for a state structure and its jurisdiction over the people it encompasses, such as Canada and the U.S., or the mainstay of an ethnic group that does not identify with the state's jurisdiction over it, such as in the case of Northern Ireland and the Mohawk nation.

Further, in keeping with a "language of liberation" (Churchill, 1994), the term *territory*, rather than *community*, will be used. The Mohawk are a nation—as such, they are the occupiers of a definable territory.

Additionally, the term *social movement* is used when referring to the Mohawk Warrior Movement. For the purpose of this study, a social movement is defined as "a collective actor constituted by individuals who understand themselves to have common interests and, for at least some part of their social existence, a common identity" (Scott, 1990:6). To further expand on this definition, a social movement is also comprised of a network of individuals and groups linked by a common identity, which affirms members' common interests. These individuals and groups are motivated by conflicting interests embedded in relations of power, to act together in pursuit of altering a social condition affecting members of the group or the position of the group in society. It is my contention that the Mohawk Warrior Movement neatly fits this definition.

Preparation for this book involved the collection and analysis of several bodies of evidence. My primary data was gathered during the period of October 1991–June 1992 and again during the period of May–August 1994. Such material was gathered principally in Canada, although portions of it were also obtained in the United States.

Using an oral history methodology, I interviewed leaders and members of the Mohawk Warrior Movement and other central figures within the Mohawk nation from three different Mohawk territories: Akwesasne, Kanehsakate, and Kahnawake. A complete list of the persons interviewed can be found in the appendix. Books, newspapers, and archival documents allowed for comparison and validation of the interviews conducted. Many primary and secondary sources were collected from the Canadian National Archives; Canadian Indian Rights Commission Library; Federal Court of Canada; Department of Indian Affairs, Canada, Research Branch; Oka Municipal Council; *Montreal Gazette*; *Malone Evening Telegram* (NY); and *Syracuse Post Standard* (NY).

Acknowledgments

Acknowledgments should do more than thank the important people in one's life; they also should pay tribute. Many individuals played an important role in this book, both directly and indirectly, over a number of years.

I am deeply grateful to members of the Mohawk nation. Without their trust and cooperation, this research would not have been possible. They allowed me to impose upon their time and privacy and, in many instances, to stir up reminders of very difficult and violent times. I can't thank them enough for the information they provided. I can only hope that I have done a worthy job in telling their story and that, in some small way, it will make a difference.

My mentors at the University of Michigan, Rosemary Sarri, Mark Chesler, Barry Checkoway, Mayer Zald, and JoEllen Shively, must be recognized both collectively and individually for their support and belief in me. In their own unique ways, each empowered me to perform the initial research from which this book was born.

A number of people and organizations also made it possible for me to complete the research for this book. The initial research was funded by a University of Michigan Rackham Dissertation Fellowship. Additional research was supported by a Canadian

Studies Faculty Research Grant, which helped provide the resources that allowed me to take this book beyond the earliest research stage, by funding several trips to Canada so I could obtain additional interview data. The Department of Ethnic Studies at Bowling Green State University also facilitated the research for this book by providing departmental resources.

My thanks also to Christine Worden, acquisitions editor, and John Sibley Butler, series editor, at State University of New York Press. Their interest in and excitement about this project encouraged me to complete the book. Additional thanks to the anonymous reviewers who provided supportive and insightful comments and questions during the revision stages of this book. Michele Lansing was incredibly thorough at copyediting. Cathleen Collins, production editor and Theresa Swierzowski, marketing, did an exceptional job.

Within the Bowling Green State University community, many individuals helped to make this book possible. My sisters in solidarity—Ellen Berry, Alice Calderonello, Lillian Aschcraft-Eason, Anne Marie Lancaster, and Opportune Zongo—were and continue to be my support system. With their wisdom and care they encouraged me not to give up. Various members of the ethnic studies department at Bowling Green State University motivated me to complete this book in a timely fashion. They all have contributed to my evolution as an academic in more ways than they could fathom. Special thanks to A. Rolando Andrade, a trusted friend and colleague as well as the most honorable person I know. He unselfishly provided me the support and encouragement I needed to trudge through the daily battles so common to untenured assistant professors in the world of academics. My graduate students, Holly Baumgartner, Tanaya Clinger, Leo Gadzekpo, Tom Lietaert, Randy Norris, Bazan Romero, Alex Udvarhelyi, and Todd Williamson, with their thirst for knowledge and willingness to learn the "real" truth about indigenous peoples, were and are the brightest scenes in this academic play.

Fay Givens, Kay McGowan, and many others within the Native American community continue to be a source of political support. I am grateful beyond words for their friendship and encouragement.

Kathy Farber, Bill Armaline, and Pam Bettis helped me keep my sense of humor and sanity during the early writing stages of this book. My heartfelt appreciation to them for their friendship and emotional, intellectual, and political support.

Seamus and Eileen Metress have given of themselves on count-less occassions to help me and my family whenever we needed it. Words cannot express the depth of my appreciation for everything they have done over the years.

Milagros Pena, my dearest friend and comrade in arms, pa-tiently listened as I worked through the process of turning a re-search project into a book. When I felt overwhelmed and sure that I could not accomplish the task, she inevitably managed to con-vince me that I could. Her encouragement has been matched by her belief in the value of my work.

Patrick McGuire is very much a part of this book, a fact for which I am grateful beyond words. On various occasions he gave up his own research time to accompany me on the long and many field trips. He was infinitely tolerant of my indulgence in numer-ous discussions with him on the topic of my research over a period of several years, having spent countless hours listening to me work out my ideas. There were times I did not know where to find the confidence to persist. He always found just the right words to mo-tivate me to complete the task. His faith in me has been matched by his commitment, and both have helped to sustain my own.

I would like to thank my parents Irene and Aldo, my brothers Steven and Robert, and my sister Laura for making me what I am today, but more importantly, for providing me with an underlying sense of security that has enabled me to reach toward what must often appear unreachable goals. To my grandmother Minnie, no longer with me, who believed I could be anything I wanted to be. If I haven't quit, it is because of you.

And last but not at all least, I acknowledge my son Seamus Daniel, who arrived just as I was beginning my second semester of teaching and who has continually challenged me, from the 1 AM and 4 AM feedings and sleepless nights to his newly found toddler freedom (more like frenzy). There were times when I thought I would never complete this book. But in the end, he helped me to keep my perspective, reminding me of what is truly important.

1

Introduction

Aboriginal-State Relations

During the past 200 years, humans have been experiencing the most powerful ethnic revival ever, a revival whose strength can be gauged by the spread of the ideology of nationalism. While there have been instances of ethnically based nationalism before the French Revolution, it is this event that made nationalism

> an almost irresistible and worldwide trend . . . the French example helped to spur ethnic nationalism elsewhere, notably in the lands conquered by Napoleon; and it was the success of the French fusion of popular sovereignty, national unity, and ethnic fraternity or identity that made it possible for other subordinated communities to entertain similar aspirations . . . the new doctrines of nationalism furnished a universal language in which to convey and legitimate ethnic aspirations, and once they began to emerge their success in one area of the globe [they] simply enhanced their appeal and potency in the eyes of new claimants. (Smith, 1981: 23–24)

The recent numerous global ethno-nationalist conflicts and mobilizations speak to the continued primacy of ethnicity, ethnic identity and boundaries, and culture for collective protest and social movement activity.

The recent struggles between indigenous peoples and the state point to the fact that indigenous nations are not immune from ethnic and nationalist conflicts similar to those that have erupted during this century in the "new" states of Africa and Asia, Europe, and the former Soviet Union, to name a few. Specifically, indigenous nations both in Canada and the United States have been and continue to be subject to conditions that elsewhere have contributed to political mobilization along ethnic and nationalist lines. Indeed, nearly five centuries of systematic socio-economic and political discrimination against aboriginal peoples have generated a sustained indigenous ethno-nationalist, political discourse as a way of mobilizing solidarity across aboriginal territories (Chartrand, 1992; Jhappan, 1993; Long, 1992). This discourse is based on claims about aboriginal peoples' right to self-determination, which includes the retaining and/or regaining of land, the right to self-government, and the recognition of their identity as nations within Canada and the United States (the latter challenges a vision of Canadian history based on "two founding peoples"). Contributing to these ethnically based nationalist claims have been the resources necessary for political mobilization—politicized ethnicity and ideology.

Aboriginal resistance to colonial domination over their land and resources has taken many forms, from the passive acts of conventional politics and legal efforts to the more aggressive acts of civil disobedience and armed uprisings. For example, the actions of members of the Mohawk nation and the Mohawk Warrior Movement exist at one end of the spectrum of political action. However, one needs to recognize that the Mohawks moved to that end because they were frustrated with the ineffectiveness of conventional channels of redress. Members of the Mohawk nation and the Mohawk Warrior Movement engaged in armed resistance in 1990 to call public attention to and garner political support for their grievances against the continued colonial domination over and seizure of their land and resources by the Canadian state.

When and how were the Mohawks motivated to accept and even embrace this "extremist" option and maintain it against such overwhelming resources and show of military force by a modern industrial nation? If anger and oppression alone led to armed uprisings, they would occur daily, as Trotsky (1965) noted. If hypocrisy incites violence, as Hannah Arendt (1970:65) argued, indigenous peoples faced with continued treaty violations would be involved in uprisings continuously. To understand these complex political and cultural processes, this book will look at the historical and contemporary conflict-relationship that exists between the Mohawk Warrior Movement and the Canadian federal and provincial state, within the context of the Mohawk nation's struggle for national self-determination. My analysis of the 1990 Mohawk-Oka conflict will reveal the significant role ideology (nationalism) and politicized ethnicity (ethnic identity and ethnic consciousness) play in social movement mobilization.

ABORIGINAL-STATE RELATIONS

The reluctance of the Canadian federal and provincial governments to acknowledge and legitimize aboriginal land claims has been a consistent historical reminder of the colonial relationship that defines aboriginal-state relations within Canada. In cases where aboriginal land claims have been recognized, such land transfers have taken place only after struggles, which in many instances erupted into violent confrontations, forcing the federal and provincial governments to return tracts of traditional land to First Nations' peoples. One such contentious land claim involved the Kanehsatake Mohawks, who in 1990 forced the Canadian federal and Quebec provincial governments to return 100 acres of traditional Mohawk land to the territory of Kanehsatake. By setting up blockades and engaging in armed confrontation, the Kanehsatake Mohawks were able to prevent the development of a golf course expansion project onto land that they have continually claimed as theirs. In an attempt to diffuse the confrontation, the Canadian federal government purchased the land from the town of Oka, Quebec, on behalf of the Kanehsatake Mohawks. However, the situation between the Kanehsatake Mohawks and the state remains problematic at best, because the federal government has yet to actually transfer the land that they purchased to the Kanehsatake Mohawks. Ethno-political conflicts such as those between the Mohawk nation and the Canadian state must be viewed within the context of the historical record of Aboriginal-Canadian state relations.

The aboriginal experience has been shaped by aboriginal struggles to survive colonial policies and practices that deliberately seek to obliterate indigenous ways of life as well as indigenous resistance to state invasions within aboriginal ancestral sovereign territories. If one maintains an understanding of the role power plays in human conflict, one is able to see that the contemporary situation of aboriginal nations is ultimately tied to the historical and socio-political reality of European (and now, Euro-Canadian and Euro-American) domination and colonialization. It is because of this reality and disparity of power that indigenous peoples continue to engage in acts of resistance to reaffirm their sovereignty and self-determination and to reclaim their sense of power. The Mohawk nation is but one of the numerous aboriginal nations struggling to survive and resist such an experience of European domination and colonization.

The struggle for aboriginal national self-determination has been a long and arduous one. For over 500 years, indigenous populations in North America have had to endure threats to their economic and political autonomy and sovereignty, the very maintenance of their cultural and political survival. Efforts by indigenous peoples to (re) gain some measure of control over their lives have been reflected in a multitude of politically significant events. Of particular importance are the politics of resistance to the encroachment of the white man, which are evident to this day. The political resistance of today has been built on the struggles of the past, placing the struggle for national self-determination in historical perspective.

Before and since the inception of the confederation of Canada, control of the land and resources within its boundaries has been the essential source of conflict between Euro-Canadians and indigenous nations. In effect, contentions over land usage and ownership have served to define the nature of Canadian-aboriginal relationships, shaping the nature of the ongoing domination and resistance to such domination.

The relationship between First Nations and the dominant society in Canada has been characterized by provincial and federal bureaucratic and administrative control over indigenous territories. This historical treatment of First Nations has greatly influenced their experiences of powerlessness and oppression. The federal and provincial governments have used policies of both annihilation and assimilation to determine the boundaries of aboriginal territories to contribute to making indigenous peoples dependent and powerless.

The most crucial element defining the powerless condition of First Nations' peoples arises from the expropriation of their lands and resources. The Canadian federal and provincial governments have controlled both aboriginal property (land) and resources and have exercised institutional power to create laws that govern the daily lives of aboriginal peoples. Native peoples have been denied traditional ritual, spiritual, and communal life and have been forced to accept an imposed government structure, replacing traditional leadership, dependence, government support, and a second-class legal status. For First Nations then, power becomes structurally grounded in relations of domination and subordination and is framed in terms of struggle between the expropriator and the expropriated. Issues of land rights as well as political sovereignty and economic self-determination thus become embedded in issues of power.

During the spring, summer, and fall of 1990, a land dispute between the Mohawk territory of Kanehsatake and the town of Oka, Quebec, Canada, emerged onto center stage of the world community, erupting into months of intense and often violent confrontation. Faced with the destruction of their ancestral burial grounds because of a proposed golf course expansion project, sovereign

Mohawk resources (land) were once more being coveted by the Canadian state for appropriation for the purpose of "economic development." As a colonized people, the Mohawk nation serves as an example of a nation of people forced to take up arms in self-defense, as a final tactic to prevent additional state appropriation of Mohawk lands.

The explosive events of the Mohawk-Oka conflict began on March 10, 1990, when a group of Mohawks from Kanehsatake began a peaceful occupation of their ancestral burial grounds to defend their land. They were attempting to block the development of a small forest bordering the Quebec resort town of Oka. It is within this forest, known as "The Pines," that the Mohawk ancestral burial ground lies. The Kanehsatake Mohawks erected a barricade to prevent the town of Oka, Quebec, from expanding its municipal golf course onto sovereign Mohawk land. As a result of social movement activity and the visibility and attention gained from that action, the Kanehsatake Mohawks succeeded in preventing the proposed golf course project from expanding onto their ancestral burial grounds.

In a narrow sense, the 1990 Mohawk-Oka conflict lasted 200 days, but this conflict was much larger than the events of those six months. Rooted in the historical reality of past injustices, the events of the 1990 Mohawk-Oka conflict epitomize and were quickly recognized by both sides as a reflection of the larger relationship and struggles that exist among aboriginal nations, ethno-nationalist movements, and the state. Thus, in addition to a struggle over ancient Mohawk land claims, the 1990 Mohawk-Oka conflict is a microcosm of both the historical realities of indigenous status in general and of the Mohawk demands for national self-determination.

Using the Mohawk-Oka conflict as the case study, this book seeks to tell a story of struggle and survival during the 1990 invasion by the Quebec provincial police and Canadian army onto Mohawk sovereign land. The story is the latest chapter in a 380-year struggle by one embattled nation fighting against violations of Mohawk sovereignty and the right to determine its political and economic destiny.

The period from 1968 through 1974 and then again in the early 1980s was a time of renewal for the Mohawk nation. A traditional Mohawk warrior society (re)emerged, combining historical traditions with twentieth-century militant strategy. Movement leaders and members began to (re)assert their Mohawk identity and voice their grievances with state repression, addressing the need for national liberation. Mohawk Warrior Movement leaders mobilized support around two themes: politicized ethnicity and ideology. To understand the motives of and effects on Mohawk Warrior Movement participants and event developments during the 1990 Mohawk-Oka conflict, one needs to understand these conditions as being important interpretive frameworks that served as rallying points which facilitated social movement mobilization during that conflict. Failure to do so would leave one in the same ethnocultural confusion and reaction that "guided" police and military action during the course of the conflict.

During the past two decades, many aboriginal nations within Canada and the United States have expressed what can only be considered a politicized ethnicity—ethnic identity and consciousness. They speak of indigenous populations as "peoples," "nations," and "nationalities" by right of the specific cultural, linguistic, territorial, and historical ties that bind them together and set them apart from others. And they have come to recognize that they need to engage in political efforts (within and outside) institutionalized processes so their identity will be recognized, respected, and legally assured. In fact, acts of political resistance have become an intrinsic part of ethnicity. This book will demonstrate the ways in which Mohawk Warrior Movement leaders developed interpretive frames which built upon that movement and its ideology. It also will show how Mohawk Warrior Movement leaders specifically cultivated a politicized ethnicity and framed the movement's ideology (nationalism) in such a manner as to facilitate member recruitment and mobilization of political capacity within the Mohawk nation and within other aboriginal nations of North America.

This idea of a "nation," a "people" that recognizes itself as distinct on the basis of shared culture and tradition, and the political principle that each national unit should have political autonomy, are among the most potent of the European ideas which have spread globally in the context of the growth of the capitalist world economy, colonialism, and the twentieth-century struggle for independence. The Mohawk nation, as do others, claims a legitimate right to use force (including armed struggle) to defend its peoples and nation, regardless of the beliefs and sanctions of the state that has asserted established claims over its autonomy and territory. As part of a larger dispossessed indigenous population that deeply embraces a nationalist ideology, the Mohawk nation points to the fact that ethnic conflict and nationalist struggles are as significant a factor in Canada and the United States as they are in certain other areas of the world.

The emergence of ethno-nationalist rhetoric within North American native rights movements of the 1970s, 1980s, and 1990s represents a capacity for mobilizing the indigenous population behind nationalist goals. It is this ethno-nationalist ideology that the leaders of the Mohawk Warrior Movement framed in ways that allowed them to mobilize participants during the 1990 Mohawk-Oka conflict. This book will show that the principal reason they were successful in their efforts to mobilize support and maintain alliances was because they adapted their ideological agenda and discourse to the predispositions and conceptions of the larger Mohawk nation.

There has yet to be a comprehensive investigation of ethnic-nationalist ideology within North American native rights movements. While there are a few studies (Hornung, 1991; Landsman, 1988; Matthiessen, 1991; Nagel, 1996; York and Pindera, 1991) that touch upon this phenomenon, they do not provide a sufficient understanding of the critical role of historical forces underlying the emergence of indigenous nationalist claims. As a result, they are not able to tell us, with any precision, how far nationalist sentiments reach into the indigenous population as a whole. However, they do present evidence that these claims are being put forward, at least by the leadership of indigenous movements. This analysis of the Mohawk Warrior Movement and its participation in the 1990 Mohawk-Oka conflict seeks ultimately to move beyond the case study. It is an attempt to lay the conceptual and theoretical groundwork for a more extensive theoretical explanation regarding the emergence of ethnic-nationalist ideology within North American native rights movements and its potential for social movement mobilization.

2

The Framing of Politicized Ethnicity and Nationalism

In the global context, there are approximately 5,000 nations (Nietschmann, 1987). Within these nations, there exists 1,600 major cultural groupings (Levinson, 1993) who speak more than 6,000 different languages (Grimes, 1988). These figures indicate the breadth and significance of global ethnic diversity. Further, since 1945, one-half of the world's states have experienced ethnic conflict (Williams, 1994).

Research on ethnicity and nationalism, including ethno-nationalist movements, has attributed this growing phenomenon of ethno-political conflict and ethno-nationalist movements to the growth of multi-ethnic states, ethnic group organization, ideological differences, economic competition and discrimination, political opportunity, the acquisition of mobilization resources by various ethnic groups, and the role of the state (Enloe, 1981; Gurr, 1993; Horowitz, 1985; Klandermans, 1984; McAdam, 1982; Nagel, 1980; Olzak, 1983; Olzak and Nagel, 1986; Tarrow, 1988; Yinger, 1985). Groups have engaged in ethno-political conflict over control of central polities, cross-national claims to territory, and autonomy or secession (Nagel, 1980:280–82). With this in mind, one can easily argue that ethno-political conflict is not new.

11

Rather, ethno-political conflict and ethno-nationalism are a re-curring and increasingly common worldwide phenomenon.

The armed uprising during the 1990 Mohawk-Oka conflict, as is the case with all acts of civil disobedience, is unique by definition. However, to understand how the Mohawk Warrior Movement emerged and mobilized its constituencies, one needs to conceptual-ize it in terms of a social movement. This requires that one first re-view the analyses of other theorists who looked at similar situations. The goal of such a review is to gain insights to guide the analysis and be able to identify indicators of various underlying conditions or processes, should such be found within the empirical analysis. Such knowledge helps to both formulate a theory and establish the grounds for confirming or challenging the applicability of the theo-ries of others. In this case, it leads toward a theory that will help understand how and why social movement activity was facilitated during the 1990 Mohawk-Oka conflict. I will argue that two highly interactive processes, politicized ethnicity (ethnic identity and con-sciousness) and ideology (nationalism), together facilitated the mo-bilization of participants and the maintenance of social movement activity.

Ted Gurr's (1993) book is a logical starting point for developing a theory of social movement activity applicable to an uprising by aboriginal peoples. He offers an explanatory model of ethno-political action that may help to understand and analyze the Mo-hawk Warrior Movement's struggle during the 1990 Mohawk-Oka conflict. In his study of ethno-political conflict and mobilization against the state, Gurr indicates that a group's historical loss of po-litical and economic autonomy, awareness of discrimination, and cultural or ethnic identity may contribute to the formulation of group grievances (p. 123). By articulating these grievances involv-ing culturally based dissatisfaction, he argues that group or move-ment leaders can mobilize and facilitate ethno-political conflict. Thus, in an analysis such as this, one should look at the content of indigenous culture, the role and content of ideology, and the role of the Mohawk Warrior Movement leaders during the 1990 Mohawk-Oka conflict.

Gurr's study further indicates that the outcome of ethno-political mobilization depends on the political opportunity factors, both internal and external, to the group, such as the extent of group grievances, the salience of group cultural or ethnic identity, the existence of networks, changing dynamics in the political environment, the power of the state and its resources, and political allies (p. 130). Thus, it is necessary to explain not only the factors that motivated participants, but also the factors or conditions that allowed participants to access opportunities, and to encourage or constrain the form and extent of extra-movement influence upon the course of event development.

While Gurr offers important insights that will help guide this book, he pays insufficient attention to the role and impact of group organization and the form and extent of resources being controlled and mobilized by the insurgent group. Further, he does not specify how history—or more specifically, a group's sense of responsibility to their history—becomes a tool or vehicle for mobilizing some (and not other) members of a large group to become part of a social movement organization. Nor does Gurr explain how and why "history" becomes a catalyst for social protest. After all, the history was always there; the existence of a social movement is intermittent.

Many social movement scholars, primarily resource mobilization theorists, have argued that the extent (length, duration, intensity, size, and distribution) of protest depends on the amount of resources under a group's collective control and the ability of leaders to allocate them in a timely and strategic manner (Gamson, 1975; McCarthy and Zald, 1977; Oberschall, 1973; Tilly, 1978 and others). In so arguing, they have identified some of the material and organizational conditions that generate and maintain social movement activity. Various studies have argued that group organization, a committed membership, kinship networks, the ability to finance activites, knowledge of the political bureaucracy and procedures, media, empathetic government officials, and public supporters can facilitate (or, by their absence, impede) the maintenance of social movement composition and the pursuit of movement goals (cf. Freeman, 1983; Zald and McCarthy, 1979; Morris 1984). While the ability to secure and mobilize resources is obviously an important part of any social movement, one cannot assume, however, that material and organizational resources are the only or primary ingredient necessary for successful social movement mobilization and maintenance; culture, specifically ideology and a politicized ethnicity, are also important, as a later discussion of Mohawk Warrior Movement activity will demonstrate.

Let me point out here that periodically, Mohawk Warrior Movement leaders have used material and organizational resources, such as group organization, a committed membership, kinship networks, the ability to finance activities, political opportunity, the media, empathetic government officials, and public supporters to garner support for and to further their goals. Although they have done so in a limited way (being members of a "traditionally" resource-deficient group), their actions fit neatly into recent models of organized protest which stress the importance of material and organizational resources (Freeman, 1983; Zald and McCarthy, 1979; Morris, 1984). However, despite this limited application of the Mohawk Warrior Movement to resource mobilization theory, several questions remain.

Resource mobilization theorists beg several questions crucial to explaining how and why groups that are deficient in material and organizational resources, such as aboriginal peoples, are able to mobilize and maintain a social movement. For example, how do ethno-political and ideological constructs become crucial components affecting the course of social movement activity? In other words, what role does politicized ethnicity (ethno-political identity and consciousness) and ideology (nationalism) play in social movement strategies? How do movement leaders resonate their constituency's cultural values and beliefs with movement goals and strategies? In other words, do movement leaders impose their values upon and create a constituency as a Leninist-like vanguard, or do they reflect and frame movement goals and strategies in manners consistent with the constituent's values? Can leaders transform the "wealth" of non-material culture or other commonalty into a resource that can facilitate political mobilization? Can culture, or manifestations of culture, specifically politicized ethnicity and ideology, catalyze and help maintain and refocus a social protest? Can something as vague as non-material culture, which only has significant meaning to mobilize a specifically affected group, become a bridge to other groups? Can it somehow be transformed into a source or conduit for the transfer of material resources to the movement?

While resource mobilization theory offers some interesting insights, its explanatory power when applied to a group which is, in traditional terms, "resource deficient," such as aboriginal peoples, is limited. And, while it may have great explanatory power in a dominant culture that is material-based, it may not be appropriate in a culture that places other values and goals ahead of and/or in place of acquisition and domination. A more cultural-sensitive and cultural-appropriate explanation is needed.

Recent literature about social movements (Benford, 1993; Brand, 1990; Eyerman and Jamison, 1991; Fantasia, 1988; Hunt and Benford, 1993; Hunt, Benford, and Snow, 1994; McAdam, 1994; Melucci, 1985, 1989; Mueller, 1987; Pena, 1995; Taylor and Whittier, 1992) has begun to offer such an additional explanation, by emphasizing the importance of cultural manifestations such as beliefs and values, identity and consciousness, ideology, and language for facilitating and maintaining social movement mobilization. Perhaps this focus on culture is a result of the recognition that social movements are not only shaped by culture, as argued by Johnston and Klandermans (1995), but that ". . . culture has always been central to the kinds of processes social movement researchers study, such as formulating grievances, defining a common identity, or developing solidarity and mobilizing action" (Swindler, 1995:30). Further, cultural manifestations—such as values, beliefs, ideology, and identity—which are processed through meaning construction, are framed and reframed by social movement leaders through discourse, consciousness-raising, and political symbols, to be complementary with the movement's goals in order to recruit member participation and facilitate and maintain mobilization (Johnston and Klandermans, 1992, 1995; Snow et al., 1986). Could particular forms of cultural expression and ideology mobilize and transform individuals into a constituency of active resistance and armed insurrection?

Snow and Benford (1988) provide a useful insight as to how nonmaterial conditions affect social movement developments. They argue that resource mobilization theory has been negligent in identifying the relationship between ideological factors and social movements. They claim that social movements frame or assign meaning to and interpret relevant events and conditions in ways that are intended to mobilize potential adherents and constituents. Movements also function as transmitters of mobilizing beliefs and ideas and are actively engaged in the production of meaning for participants, antagonists, and observers (197–198). The usefulness of movement leaders, in general, to protest movements depends on their ability to mobilize constituents. Stated succinctly, social movements are "producers of meaning" in that they become conduits for the articulation of (constituency) values and beliefs, goals, and grievances (Klandermans, 1989:9), which are conveyed through an ideology that is used by movement leaders to facilitate member participation. In this way ". . . framing efforts can be thought of as acts of cultural appropriation, with movement leaders seeking to tap highly resonant ideational strains . . . as a way of galvanizing activism" (McAdam, 1994:37–38).

In order to analyze how culture affects action, one needs to specify concepts and indicators of its form and influence. My theoretical point of departure for this effort is Tucker's (1989) conception of ideology: ideology is a product of cultural traditions. Here I refer to a framework through which values and beliefs, goals, and grievances are interpreted. In other words, this book shows that ideology is immersed in the language and culture of the constituency. Thus, for protest action to take place, the ideology of the movement must be in some form of alignment with that of its constituents. Movement ideologies must be understood in both the material and ideological context of the societies in which they emerge (Ferree and Miller, 1985:43). Did the particular ideology of the Mohawk Warrior Movement play a significant role in both articulating group values and beliefs, goals, and grievances and in calling individuals to action? Can we build on Tucker's definition of ideology and Snow and Benford's insight about ideological frames and frame resonance to explain how the specific content of Aboriginal culture can facilitate the armed uprising and successes of a resource-deficient aboriginal group in particular and of ethno-political insurgency in general? These insights would seem to indicate that any analysis of the 1990 Mohawk uprising needs to focus on the culture of the Mohawk nation and Mohawk Warrior Movement members.

The heart of culture is a history of shared events and meanings. Thus, a focus on the history of previous historical conflicts is a logical prerequisite to an explanation of how the content of culture affects a contemporary struggle. That focus allows identification of whether history serves as conceptual or interpretive framework in which participants act upon deeply held beliefs. It also will provide insights into what symbolic (as well as particular) meanings exist which could be used to encourage participation in protest activity. By examining Mohawk land claims from 1608 to the 1990 Mohawk uprising, one also can identify the changing (and constant) content of aboriginal/state relationships in general. By examining the unfolding of this history, one can learn the various and changing impacts of external factors which have affected that history—and which may serve as an ongoing lesson in the consciousness of leaders and participants. This examination will show how external factors have shaped the socio-political conditions affecting the contemporary Mohawk nation. Since that history has a specific reference point, the Mohawks, it will determine the extent to which "history" itself might serve as a rallying point for social movement participation, mobilization, and maintenance, and whether history could help guide the actions taken by the Mohawk Warrior Movement during the 1990 Mohawk-Oka conflict.

Stated directly, did a knowledge of the 380-year history of land theft by the state create among Mohawks a common lens to interpret events? Did the fact that it was a land claim, a source of historical struggle and not some other economic grievance, constitute or create a sense of obligation or responsibility within the group that otherwise would have laid dormant? Could this be one of the reasons why the Mohawks were willing to prevent further expropriation by the state by armed force if necessary? Such a historical analysis also may help to answer larger questions, such as, how does a sense of history become translated into action? Are people motivated by history because it seems to represent a legal precedent creating the basis for material gain, a materialist motive, or are they motivated by culturally specific factors such as family obligation, self- and group identity, and respect?

Most studies set the historical backdrop for a contemporary conflict and treat history like geography, as only a loose contextual factor. But this book differs in that it will examine whether "history" is a motive, a part of the mobilization, a facet of the strategies, a key to understanding the goals, and a crucial insight into the heart and soul of the Mohawk nation and the Mohawk Warrior Movement. Further, this book asks whether "history" is somehow causal and not just a contingent pressure on contemporary decision-making.

How does history become "operationalized"? One possible explanation lies in collective identity formation. Collective identity derives from the shared experiences and beliefs, common interests, and solidarity of individuals (Boggs, 1986; Cohen, 1985; Epstein, 1990; Melucci, 1985; Morris and Mueller, 1992; Taylor, 1989; Taylor and Whittier, 1992), which are developed, redefined, and solidified through interactions within the social networks of a social movement (Melucci, 1994).

Collective identity implies that individuals see themselves as part of a group (Touraine, 1985; Melucci, 1989). This sense of "we" is a product of common experiences constructed through a common history of oppression and domination and a shared structural location. In other words, history as part of the stories of peoples' lives is part of personal identity formation. And to the extent that the content of that history is shared, it is part of the content of group, or collective, identity. Ethnic minority identity is distinctly separate from and in opposition to the dominant society and its legalistic values. As such, personal and collective identity formation "transforms" history into motive for action and constitutes a partial strategy for action, in that it encourages mobilization in support of that oppositional identity.

However, Klandermans (1994) argues that this sense of collective identity is not a fixed phenomenon but rather is transient in that

> . . . the collective identity of movement participants changes over time as the life cycle of a movement evolves. . . . One of the vehicles for the transformation of collective identity is the changing composition of the body of activists within a movement. . . . With a new wave of activists entering a new configuration of shared beliefs evolves. The result may be a transformed collective identity. (p. 169)

If this argument about the role of collective identity within social movements is to be supported herein, then one would expect to see that the collective identity of the protest participants changed over the duration of the 1990 Mohawk-Oka conflict as the influx of Mohawk Warrior Movement leaders into the conflict evolved.

Further, if history and collective identity are significant factors explaining the mobilization and participation of individuals and influencing the conduct of the struggle, one should be able to explain the processes by which this occurs. Again, Snow and Benford's (1988) theory of frame analysis provides a possible answer. They note that an ideological frame both motivates participation and allows movement leaders to rededicate and refocus efforts to contend with the changing content of the social movement and strategic conditions of the social struggle. Treating their insight as a point to be demonstrated and not assumed, but looking for possible indicators of their theory, there are several potential conditions that might be construed as indicating that history is a motive for action.

Among these are emphasis by participants on history as a source of personal responsibility or obligation, a source (and site) of personal and/or collective values, or direct references to history as identity.

These basic questions suggest that while history may explain the participation of Mohawks, this explanation can only explain part of what happened during the 1990 Mohawk-Oka conflict. Much of the motivation and mobilization that occurred is logically beyond both the resource-based theory and the history as motive explanation. This point suggests that another factor (and a more broad synthetic theory) is needed to augment and complement the "history" as (partial) explanation of social movement participation.

Can aspects of the Mohawk Warrior Movement ideology be a factor in winning supporters, especially among non-Mohawk aboriginals and society at large? To determine this, one needs to examine the content and implications of that ideology. One also needs to examine and specify how and why the content of that ideology might motivate actors other than those directly affected by the extension of the golf course, and their immediate family and community members. One needs to examine whether the belief in Mohawk national self-determination or Mohawk nationalism was a key factor which spurred the widespread mobilization of support during the 1990 Mohawk-Oka conflict.

Benford (1993) and Hunt and Benford (1993) have noted the importance of language as a factor mobilizing and guiding participants in social movements. While they describe dissident movements of and within the dominant society, their basic insight deserves and will receive investigation herein. However, consistent with an earlier noted insight about the content of native identity, I will pay special attention to the different content and impact of language within this opposition culture. For example, I will examine how, why, and with what effects movement leaders used the language of liberation—the ideology of Mohawk nationalism—to articulate group grievances against state repression. Did leaders deliberately (or inadvertently) nurture and capitalize on an ideological interpretive frame, "nationalism," to assign a greater meaning to movement participation and protest activity?

One also needs to determine whether Mohawk Warrior Movement leaders knew that their ability to mobilize their Mohawk supporters, their extended social networks among other Iroquois, and the potential capacity of other aboriginal allies and even non-aboriginal supporters, depended on the resonance of movement goals with their constituent's traditionally held beliefs of themselves as a people—the belief that the Mohawk people constitute a sovereign nation. How important was the demarcation of territorial boundaries? Was the stated goal of reestablishing Mohawk control over Mohawk political and economic affairs a crucial factor in mobilization? Or was it the language frame, the explanation of the meaning of these and other events, that was the key to encouraging the mobilization of political capacity in support of the Mohawk Warrior Movement and their struggle during the 1990 Mohawk-Oka conflict?

Did Mohawk Warrior Movement leaders use this ideology to mobilize other protest constituencies by willfully framing their actions and goals in manners that allowed non-Mohawks to justify participation in direct-action protest? Did this rhetoric create or constitute a legitimate rationale for joining or supporting the Mohawk Warrior Movement? Was Mohawk nationalism an example of leaders providing "the kind of ideological package that successfully resonated with larger cultural themes" (Gamson 1988: 227)—themes that resonated not only through the oppositional aboriginal culture but also through significant segments of the dominant culture?

A search for evidence in support of Gamson's view requires exploring the emergence and application of ideological symbols of the interpretive framework of nationalism. This exploration would include the strategic and symbolic impacts of actions such as establishing group and national boundaries by creating barricades and blockading bridges. Did these assert and/or affirm Mohawk nationalism? If previously uninvolved Mohawks, including

those who were critical of the Mohawk Warrior Movement, became motivated to join the protest after participation was equated
with nationhood, then this would further indicate the importance
of the nationhood frame.

One also needs to identify whether these symbols as frames
were resonated. Demonstrating that the composition and rationale for such actions changed in response to different conditions
at crucial periods would support the thesis of the centrality of the
ideology of nationalism as a factor in mobilization and maintenance of this movement. If it can be shown that it became a
method of gaining access to otherwise nonexistent resources, such
as media, extended social networks, political influence, etc., that
would further strengthen these claims.

If I can show that Mohawk Warrior Movement leaders provided
what Ash (1972) calls a "cognitive framework" and what Snow
and Benford (1988) call an "interpretive framework" for opposition and resistance, then it is appropriate to argue that Mohawk
nationalism (in particular and politicized ethnicity in general)
was a causal factor or motive for mobilizing potential actors for
social movement activity. If the importance of ideology is shown,
this would suggest that the adaptation of cultural principles to
protest action depended upon the interpretive skills of the Mohawk Warrior Movement leaders, as they translated and articu-
lated events, grievances, and their meaning for their supporters,
by providing an explanation that was perceived as consistent with
the ideal values of the larger Mohawk society.

These various ideas present a sense of what might have occurred during the 1990 Mohawk-Oka conflict and provide a basis
for identifying significant factors, analyzing impacts, and specify-
ing interactive factors within the concrete and often chaotic
events of this half-year-long struggle. As will become apparent, I
believe that a combination of the insights and synthesis of these
theoretical approaches is important to understanding the 1990
Mohawk uprising.

In part, because of the nature of aboriginal culture and the history and material conditions of those groups, a particular combi-

nation of politicized ethnicity and an ideology of nationalism were essential preconditions and catalysts for the mobilization and maintenance of the insurrection. Further, by their resonance they created the basis for securing some of the material resources that were crucial for a resource-deficient group to continue their struggle. Learning how these factors come together to facilitate protest activity in this particular case can also lend some insight into the larger issue of ethno-political conflict.

Before an in-depth examination and analysis of the importance of these material and non-material resources to the 1990 Mohawk-Oka conflict can take place, one needs to understand two distinct but interconnected histories; an overview of Mohawk history as it pertains to that conflict, and the particular history of the emergence and development of the Mohawk Warrior Movement.

3

Nations at War

History in Perspective

> Everyone thinks that July 11, it just started. It didn't. July 11 was the wall that our back could not push through anymore. You think this came out of nowhere? What, that one day we said we are going to put up barricades? This wasn't something new. It went back hundreds of years. It wasn't a new struggle, it was part of an old one, a continuous one. Look at the history, it's there. . . .
>
> —Debra Etienne

This statement reflects the importance of the history of past struggles as a motive for members of the Mohawk nation to participate in contemporary struggles, specifically the conflict that occured over the long-standing land dispute between the Mohawk nation and the state (both the Quebec provincial and Canadian federal governments) in 1990. Through a sense of collective history, people of like mind and experience come together to give political definition to their activities.

This chapter sets the historical stage of this case study so one may understand the jurisdictional issues that contributed to the 1990 Mohawk-Oka conflict. By doing so, one will gain both a greater understanding of how history served as a rallying point for mobilization and how history guided actions taken by the Mohawk Warrior Movement during the spring, summer, and fall of 1990. By presenting the historical events which have preceded and contributed to the land dispute between the Mohawk nation and the state allows one to understand the motivations, ideology, and tactics of the movement and the extent to which this event was part of an ongoing struggle.

The events of the Mohawk-Oka conflict were not isloated. Rather, they were preceded by a 380-year struggle against violations of Mohawk sovereignty. Taking a few acres for a golf course seems unimportant to most non-native citizens, however, land seizures by the state have continuously claimed more land from a constantly shrinking property acreage. Canadian provincial and federal government seizures of Mohawk territory for bridges, roads, power lines, seaways, and golf courses have occurred for decades.

THE BATTLEGROUND

At the confluence of the Ottawa and St. Lawrence Rivers is the resort town of Oka, Quebec, and the neighboring Mohawk territory of Kanehsatake. With its 3,000 residents, Oka (once referred to as "Lake of Two Mountains" by the first white settlers, the priests of the Seminary of St. Sulpice) is a picturesque farming town nestled in rolling forested hills twenty-five miles west of Montreal (Canada, 1991). Because of its location on the river, Oka has become a tourist and recreational town during the summer months. Many Oka residents involved in tourism and tourism-related businesses are of French-Canadian ancestry.

Amidst the township of Oka is Kanehsatake ("Place of the Crusty Sand," the name given to the Mohawk settlement by their ancestors). Kanehsatake, currently a native settlement of 1,700

Mohawks, is one of seven territories in Canada and the United States which is part of the Mohawk nation (Canada, 1992). The Mohawk territory of Kanehsatake does not have reserve status, or as Americans would say, it is not a reservation.

Rather, the Kanehsatake territory is composed of parcels of land, made up of Mohawk households and businesses which are interspersed among French-Canadian farms. This condition is the result of one-time Mohawk land having been sold by the Sulpician Order of Priests to individual settlers, the English Crown, and the Canadian federal government. More than two-thirds of the Kanehsatake Mohawks reside on federally owned land, while less than one-third reside on Crown-owned lots (Canada, 1992). Because the Mohawks are so geographically dispersed, they are without a unified geographic base (an area of contiguous properties constituting a duly authorized jurisdiction that might formally be deemed a Mohawk community).

During the spring, summer, and fall of 1990, a land dispute between the Mohawk nation and the town of Oka, Quebec, erupted into weeks of intense and often physically violent confrontation. The events of this conflict epitomized the larger relationship that existed between First Nations and the government of Canada. Thus, in addition to a struggle over ancient Mohawk land claims, the Mohawk-Oka conflict was a microcosm of both the historical realities of indigenous status in general and of the Mohawk demands for nationhood, which includes economic self-determination and self-government.

The explosive events of the Mohawk-Oka conflict began on March 10, 1990, with the erection of a peaceful barricade within the boundaries of an active Mohawk cemetery at Kanehsatake. The barricades were erected in an attempt to prevent the town of Oka from expanding its municipal golf course onto the burial ground. The Pine Hill Cemetery (adjacent to the Oka Golf Club's parking lot and driveway) and the neighboring "Pines" (a forest of white pine trees bordering the town of Oka, just west of the cemetery) are the heart of the territory that the Kanehsatake Mohawks have claimed as their own for more than 300 years.

The town of Oka has established a claim to "The Pines," using it as a municipal park. However, despite not having legal (as defined by the state) ownership of "The Pines" and the cemetery, the Mohawks assert that they never surrendered their aboriginal rights to the land and claim also that all of the Lake of Two Mountains land, including the town of Oka, is Mohawk territory. It was in this setting and over this land that the 1990 Mohawk-Oka conflict and armed resistance was waged.

During the seventy-eight-day, armed standoff, in which a Quebec provincial police officer was killed and many on both sides of the dispute were injured, provincial and federal officials negotiated with the Mohawks for the removal of the barricades. The result of the armed standoff and the negotiations was the purchase of the land in question by the federal government from the town of Oka, on behalf of the Mohawk nation.

In a narrow sense, the 1990 Mohawk-Oka conflict lasted 200 days (from the March 10 barricade to the July 11 pre-dawn raid on the Mohawk barricades until September 26, when the last of the remaining warriors left Kanehsatake), but it was much larger than the events of those six months. Mohawk respondents trace the conflict as far back as the latter part of the eighteenth century and as recent as the land claims filed by the Mohawk nation in 1975 and 1977.

THE CONFLICT IN HISTORICAL PERSPECTIVE

The Mohawk people of Kanehsatake have been systematically struggling to regain control over their ancestral lands since the encroachment of the missionary priests from St. Sulpice in 1717. As Curtis Nelson, a Kanehsatake Mohawk and one of the first participants in the 1990 Mohawk-Oka conflict, testified before the Standing Committee on Aboriginal Affairs:

> While it is true that several Mohawk families who had converted to Christianity were relocated to the Kanehsatake region by the Sulpicians in the eighteenth century, it is

equally true that Mohawks occupied the area prior to their arrival, along with citizens of the Algonquin and Nipissing nations who were under our protection. Historical evidence does exist to document our prior occupation. Many attempts were made to remove us from our homeland. In the late nineteenth century several Mohawk families, most of whom had come with the Sulpicians, were coerced and tricked into what is now known as Gibson Reserve, north of Toronto. The Algonquin and Nipissings also had accepted land elsewhere, but the Mohawks, who had always been there, refused to leave our traditional homelands. Efforts to remove all of our people persisted, but to no avail. There are many people in Kanehsatake who have stories of how the Sulpicians and your [the Canadian] government tried to force out our ancestors. (March 12, 1991, p. 54)

Thus, in the minds of the Mohawks, the territory of Kanehsatake has never belonged to either the Quebec provincial or Canadian federal government, legally or historically. Rather, it is located on traditional aboriginal land that belongs to the Mohawk nation.

Despite the longtime settlement of Mohawks in the area, Mohawk lands in the valley along the St. Lawrence River were claimed by King Louis IV of France as part of "New France" (now Quebec) in 1608 (DIAND 1990; Francis, 1983; Miller, 1991; Trigger, 1977; Villeneuve & Francis, 1984). The Kanehsatake Mohawks' struggle over land rights began in the fall of 1717. At that time, the land on the eastern shore of Lake of Two Mountains (now Oka) was granted in trust by the governor of New France, Philippe de Rigaud de Vaudreuil, (on behalf of King Louis XV) to the Seminary of St. Sulpice of Paris, a Catholic missionary order (Lacan, 1876; Miller, 1991; Trigger, 1977; York & Pindera, 1991). The Sulpicians used the land granted them to set up a mission to convert the indigenous inhabitants to Roman Catholicism. In 1733, the Sulpician Order of Priests petitioned for a second land grant to provide a larger land base for converting the Mohawks to Catholicism, and in 1735 their petition was approved (Lacan, 1876; Lacoste, 1880; York & Pindera, 1991). Both land concessions were granted "in trust to" the Sulpicians on behalf of the Mohawks who became part of the mission. In addition, if the Mohawks left the mission, it was understood that the title of the land would revert back to the King of France.

In 1736, those Mohawks who were converted to Catholicism by the Sulpician priests built a permanent agricultural settlement near the church (Francis, 1983; Ornstein, 1973). They began farming the land and planted the forest (known as "The Pines") that the town of Oka, 250 years later, would try to turn into a golf course.

Despite the Sulpician's use of the land for a Catholic mission, the Mohawks claim the land was part of their territory long before the Sulpician priests settled there and that they were the earliest known inhabitants of the region. Such a claim is important because in accordance with the Canadian land claim process, indigenous peoples must prove they have occupied the land in question since pre-Euro-Canadian contact, or "time immemorial," in order to have their land rights recognized (Miller, 1991). Further, the Mohawks believe they retained their land rights as in accordance with an agreement marked by the Two Dog Wampum treaty belt.

It is an Iroquois tradition to document treaties with belts made of shells (wampum). The Mohawks created a wampum belt to commemorate their agreement with the Sulpician Order of Priests. That belt, they claim, signifies that the Seminary of St. Sulpice could build their mission, but that the Lake of Two Mountains area would always be Mohawk territory. As York and Pindera (1991) describe, the Two Dog Wampum treaty belt

> depicted men on either side of a cross—a symbol of the Mohawk's adherence to the faith of the Sulpician priests. A long white band was meant to symbolize the limits of their territory. At each end of the belt was a figure of a dog, who was to stand guard over the land, barking warnings to the Mohawks if anyone disturbed them in their lands. (p. 86–7)

However, the agreement made between the Mohawks and the Sulpicians, as represented in the belt, was not honored consistent with the Mohawk understanding.

Following the British conquest of New France in 1760 (the French and Indian War), the Mohawks were permitted to remain on the lands they inhabited unless they formally relinquished possession of those lands to the King of England (Villeneuve & Francis, 1984, York & Pindera, 1991). Such guarantees were later confirmed in the Royal Proclamation of 1763, leading the Mohawks of Lake of Two Mountains to believe that their land rights to the territory would be recognized (Getty & Lussier, 1983). The Royal Proclamation of 1763 is considered by First Nations across Canada to be a legal agreement confirming their land rights. However, the Seminary of St. Sulpice continued to assert its ownership rights to the land, while the Mohawks continued to challenge that assertion, maintaining that Lake of Two Mountains was Mohawk territory. Thus, the original petition for a land grant and trustee rights had become "translated" or "transferred" into a claim of property rights.

To settle the question of ownership of Lake of Two Mountains lands, the Legislature of Lower Canada (now Quebec) passed an act known as the Ordinance of 1840. The Ordinance of 1840 gave the Seminary of St. Sulpice ownership title to the land and trusteeship over the Mohawk settlements. It cited that any original land rights that might have existed had been eliminated by government actions, beginning with the land grants made by King Louis XV of France in the eighteenth century (Daniels, 1980; DIAND, 1990; Pariseau, 1974). The Ordinance of 1840, explicitly recognizing the Sulpician's ownership of Oka, would be the first of many decisions made by the state that would refuse to legally recognize the legitimacy of Mohawk land claims. The Sulpician Order of Priests' ownership of Mohawk lands at Oka was again upheld in 1867 with confederation: British North America became the Dominion of Canada under the British Crown (Daniels, 1980; Pariseau, 1974).

The Mohawks, however, continued to assert their aboriginal rights to their land and, in 1868, petitioned the federal government to recognize their territorial rights. After considering the legality of the Sulpician land grants, the Superintendent General of

Indian Affairs, William Spragge, ruled that Mohawk rights to the land had never been eliminated (Daniels, 1980; York & Pindera, 1991). He also ruled that the land grants made to the seminary of St. Sulpice and the Jesuits at Kahnawake were similar. This ruling was important for the Kanehsatake Mohawks because in the case of Kahnawake, the courts had ruled that the Jesuit priests were not the absolute owners of the land, but rather were administrators on behalf of the Kahnawake Mohawks.

In addition, the Superintendent General of Indian Affairs suggested that the lands of Lake of Two Mountains be transferred from the seminary of St. Sulpice to the Crown, to be held in trust for the Mohawks (Daniels, 1980). However, despite this favorable decision and the close parallels with the Kahnawake Mohawk land claim decision, Secretary of State Hector Langevin, satisfied with the validity of the seminary's title to the land, ruled that the Mohawks had no rights to the land at Lake of Two Mountains, upholding the Sulpician's property rights (Canada, 1868; Lacoste, 1880).

Within a year, in late 1869, the Sulpician priests were selling large parcels of land to white settlers (Villeneuve & Francis, 1984; York & Pindera, 1991). As a result, in 1875 the area had become so populated with white settlers (French Canadians who had settled on what had previously been recognized as Mohawk lands) that the town of Oka was incorporated as a municipality (Daniels, 1980; Francis, 1983; York & Pindera, 1991).

In 1878, the Mohawks once again petitioned the federal government to recognize their claim to the land. After reviewing their petition, the Minister of Justice ruled in favor of the Seminary of St. Sulpice, concluding that

> the title of the Corporation of the Seminary of Montreal had conferred upon the Sulpicians the sole absolute owners of the property known as the Lake of Two Mountains. Consequently, the Oka Indians have not and never had any lawful proprietary claim in the property of the said land. It can therefore be seen from the above decisions, as well as from

the opinions expressed by the highest authorities in the land, that the Seminary of St. Sulpice has the absolute right to the property of the Lake of Two Mountains, and that the Indians have no proprietary rights in this land. (Canada, Indian Affairs, 1878)

In 1908, the Mohawks yet again initiated proceedings against the Sulpician priests, with respect to title of the lands at Oka (Daniels, 1980). Quebec Superior Court Judge J. Hutchinson dismissed the action in 1910 on the grounds that the Mohawks did not prove that they had occupied the lands as proprietors (DIAND, 1910; Quebec Superior Court, 1910). The Mohawks appealed the decision and eventually their petition was heard before the Judicial Committee of the Privy Council in England. Canadian native land claims had to be heard before a British council because the Mohawks were appealing to regain Crown-owned land. The Canadian federal government did not purchase portions of the Crown-owned land until 1945.

In 1912, the Privy Council in England rejected the Mohawk claim, upholding the seminary's title to the land. Citing the Ordinance of 1840, they ruled that Aboriginal title to land was limited and could be abolished unilaterally by legislative action (Daniels, 1980; DIAND, 1990; Miller, 1991). Although the Privy Council ruled that the land belonged to the seminary and not to the Mohawks, it suggested, however, that there might be a trust-trustee relationship which it (the Privy Council) was not able to examine in the petition as presented (ibid.). The Canadian Department of Indian Affairs took the position that the 1912 decision had settled the issue of land ownership. And for more than thirty years, the Department of Indian Affairs did not act, propose, or lobby for the introduction of legislation that would lead to a solution to this legal conflict.

In 1945, the federal government, concerned that the seminary was continuing to sell parcels of land at Oka and wanting to protect the Mohawks, attempted to settle the long-standing land claim dispute between the Kanehsatake Mohawks and the Sulpicians. The Canadian federal government purchased what was left from the Seminary of St. Sulpice, agreeing to assume all of the seminary's obligations toward the Mohawks (Daniels, 1980; Morrison & Wilson, 1991). The Mohawks were then given "certificates of possession" that guaranteed their right to remain on the land, and the federal government negotiated an agreement with the town of Oka to pay annual property taxes on this land (Daniels, 1980; York & Pindera, 1991). According to York and Pindera (1991), 132 lots (about one and one-half square miles, or 1percent of the original combined land grants of 1717 and 1735 made to the Seminary of St. Sulpice), dispersed throughout the town of Oka, remained from Mohawk land at Lake of Two Mountains (p. 102).

However, no legal reserve was put into place. As a result, the 1,700 Kanehsatake Mohawks have no reserve status. And, once again, the Mohawks maintained their claim to all of Oka. They argued that the federal government had purchased the land illegally, since it was not the Sulpician's to sell. In 1947, the federal government sold the very same land they had purchased from the seminary two years earlier to the town of Oka, Quebec (Daniels, 1980).

During the 1950s, the town of Oka drew up plans to develop the land to be used for public recreation. In 1959, the Quebec legislature passed a bill enabling the municipality of Oka to create a nine-hole golf course adjacent to the territory of Kanehsatake on land claimed by the Mohawks (Daniels, 1980). To protest the development of the golf course, the Kanehsatake Mohawks employed the services of a lawyer, Emile Colas. Representing the Mohawks' interests in Ottawa, he attempted to stop the golf course development. However, he would not be victorious, as the Canadian federal government refused to recognize any Mohawk ancestral title to the land (Rochon, 1991). During that same year, the municipality of Oka leased part of "The Pines," just west of the town to a private corporation, the Club de golf Oka Inc., to build a private, members-only, nine-hole golf course. With each decision and subsequent resale and/or lease, the clarity of the original land claims was further immersed into a legal quagmire. And, the definition and attribution of non-native ownership became further locked in the legal and social fabric of non-native life and conventionality.

As far as the Mohawks were concerned, the conflict over the status of Mohawk land at Oka remained in place. Now, the fight for their land rights would be waged against private landowners and the municipality of Oka. In 1975, the Mohawk nation at Kanehsatake, Kahnawake, and Akwesasne filed a "comprehensive land claim" with the Canadian federal and Quebec provincial governments, reasserting their rights to lands along the St. Lawrence and Ottawa Rivers, a large area which included the Lake of Two Mountains lands (DIAND, 1990; Hutchins, 1977; Miller, 1991; York & Pindera, 1991). According to Canadian federal land claims policy, a comprehensive land claim is a legal claim submitted by a First Nation, demonstrating that the land being claimed is not covered by a treaty and that aboriginal title has not been superseded by law. Further, any comprehensive land claim submitted by a First Nation must include evidence that the land has been occupied since "time immemorial" (Miller, 1991, p. 304).

Four months after the Mohawk nation submitted their claim, it was rejected by the Department of Indian Affairs and Northern Development (DIAND) on the grounds that the Mohawks could not prove that they had occupied the disputed territory continuously to the exclusion of others since "time immemorial" (DIAND, 1990; York & Pindera, 1991). DIAND further ruled that any aboriginal land rights that may have existed were made void by the land concessions granted to the Seminary of St. Sulpice, first by the French and later upheld by the English Crown and subsequent government actions (ordinances and statutes) (DIAND, 1990; Hutchins, 1977).

In 1977, the Kanehsatake Mohawks, not willing to surrender their aboriginal land rights, filed a "specific land claim" for legal rights to their Lake of Two Mountains lands (DIAND, 1990; Miller, 1991; York & Pindera, 1991). A specific land claim is a legal claim submitted by a First Nation, demonstrating that there is a violation of specific existing treaty provisions (Miller, 1991, p. 304). Because the Mohawk nation never formally engaged in a treaty with the government regarding Lake of Two Mountains land, DIAND ruled that the government was not in violation of any agreement (DIAND, 1990; York & Pindera, 1991). However, by the same token, if no treaty was established, then the Mohawk claim that they never surrendered their land by treaty or other means must be taken into consideration.

The Kanehsatake Mohawks asserted that their aboriginal rights to this land, as in accordance with the Proclamation of 1763, had never been nullified by the government, nor had they surrendered them. In 1986, after almost a decade of deliberations and appeals, DIAND again rejected the land claim filed by the Mohawk nation, on the grounds that it did not meet the federal government's criteria for "specific land claims" (DIAND, 1990; York & Pindera, 1991). DIAND further ruled that the federal government had no legal obligation to recognize Mohawk land rights to Lake of Two Mountains. The issue of Mohawk land rights to Lake of Two Mountains would not come up again for almost four years, not until the town of Oka and Oka Golf Club's joint expansion project, which would ultimately spark the Mohawk-Oka conflict of 1990.

History is more than background data. Several generations of Mohawks have fought and refought the legal battle for the Lake of Two Mountains land. Assertion of land claims themselves are part of culture and lore—part of the thread binding the various Mohawk clans into a community. The history of this land and of the struggles are told and retold to each generation at family gatherings and community and religious events. Listening to the members of Kanehsatake, one is impressed and surprised at how well-known and widely disseminated the history of this land is and how familiar the Mohawks are with government machinations. The events become a backdrop against which the differential values, beliefs, logics, and culture of native peoples, relative to non-native peoples and their institutions and their hegemonic culture, are explained and taught to subsequent generations.

History is the unbroken thread from the past and a path to a collective future. It is a source of obligation and sense of responsibility that influences perceptions or lenses through which people interpret subsequent developments. It is a source of identity, identity distinctly apart from and in opposition to the dominant society and its legalistic values, as well as a motive and strategy for action to protect that identity.

SUMMARY

The historical events presented represent more than a dispute over parcels of land. A review of the history explains the underlying processes and allows non-native peoples to understand why and how the historical context helped shape the mobilization process of the Mohawk Warrior Movement and guide their actions (and those of their socially networked allies) during the Mohawk-Oka conflict in 1990. The historical processes and impacts of the expropriation of Mohawk land (presented herein) are significant because, as one shall see in the subsequent chapters, they are what motivated and shaped Mohawk Warrior Movement participation and protest action during the Mohawk-Oka conflict of 1990. Specifically, Mohawk Warrior Movement leaders capitalized on a sense of responsibility to history, to cultivate commitment to the movement and participation in the conflict.

Collective history shapes collective consciousness. Through a sense of collective history, individuals and groups become aware of who they are. Specifically, I argue that identity and consciousness formation are part of an awakening process which is, in part, constructed through a sense of history. For First Nations, this sense of collective history, which is rooted in the historical reality of past injustices, can shape strategies of resistance.

It has been the intent of this chapter to set the historical stage in order to understand the contemporary Mohawk-Oka conflict. The next two chapters trace the emergence of the Mohawk Warrior Movement and the mobilization of Mohawk militancy.

4

Culture, Ideology, and Organizational Formation

The Rise of the Mohawk Warrior Movement

> Being a member of the Mohawk Warriors carries with it certain responsibilities . . . not only the every day operations of the Movement but the Mohawk nation as well. Our goal has always been the future of the Mohawk nation . . . that is our responsibility. And that's what has united everyone . . . our responsibility to the nation, to Mohawk nationhood. . . . It's a responsibility to history and cultural survival, and it's a responsibility to political survival . . . and it's a responsibility we do not take lightly.
>
> —Allan Delaronde,
> Mohawk Warrior Movement leader

This statement reflects the ideological justification of the Mohawk Warrior Movement. It succinctly summarizes the merging of responsibility to history and to cultural heritage, with political interests. For movement members, this is the basis of the ideology of Mohawk nationalism.

39

The previous chapter focused on the historical events (a history of land expropriation) that contributed to the Mohawk-Oka conflict, which took place during the spring, summer, and fall of 1990. This chapter, as well as the next chapter, will review and analyze the emergence and development of the Mohawk Warrior Movement from 1968 to 1990. The primary goal is to highlight the origin and development of the ideology of the Mohawk Warrior Movement, which subsequently influenced the trajectory of the 1990 Mohawk resistance. Once again, one will see the importance of history for protest activity.

BIRTH OF A MOVEMENT

The Mohawk Warrior Movement emerged from the social turmoil and demands for social justice that existed in the late 1960s and early 1970s in both the United States and Canada. The grassroots civil rights movements of blacks, women, Chicanos, and so on prompted many First Nation peoples to rethink the meaning of their identities. As a result, they subsequently began to mobilize.

Although First Nation peoples were influenced by these civil rights movements, the native rights movement originated from a different historical, legal, property, and political status. While it is true that blacks, Chicanos, and women were oppressed, as were First Nation peoples, the latter, however, differed in that they once had been land owners and had legal documents granting them this status, although their title to the land was later ignored. This gave them claim to the land and in some ways allowed their struggle to be a combination of civil, legal, and property rights, a somewhat different situation than other oppressed groups. Also, their decision-making had been usurped or preempted by paternalistic agencies (such as the Bureau of Indian Affairs, or the B.I.A.). Thus, once recognized as cognizant actors (rather never having been full members of society) and having signed legal treaties, or having treaties signed by individuals the dominant society's government claimed were representatives of indigenous nations, they had grounds for challenging the legality and propriety of paternalism and its effects.

If a legal decision had occurred which established that indigenous peoples were never responsible actors, this would throw all treaties and decisions made with them involving property rights and custodial authority into question. Because such a decision was never enacted, the courts and government agencies had to deal with the demands of First Nations peoples within a different social, political, legal, and economic context than other oppressed groups. Otherwise, they risked undermining their own authority and the legal basis of property relations. This contradiction and history of expropriation constitutes an opportunity that makes aboriginal mobilization easier and provides a different opportunity structure for native groups, relative to other oppressed groups. It affected the origin, development, and subsequent symbols; the methods of mobilization; and the outcomes of struggles by the native rights social movement.

One of the most influential groups to emerge was the American Indian Movement (AIM). The AIM engaged in organized struggle to (re) gain and maintain control over Aboriginal rights. Many Mohawks were members of the AIM. Their knowledge of history, and experience with protest gained as members of the AIM, as well as their organizational and strategic expertise, were passed on to Mohawk Warrior Movement leaders. As Harold Oakes, a Mohawk Warrior Movement member who is also a member of the Akwesasne Warrior Society, and whose cousin was a member of the AIM during the early '70s, remarked:

> We watched and learned from what they did. We began to see that what they were doing on a bigger scale needed to be done here. The issues were the same, only more localized. We figured that if native peoples worked on both fronts, the AIM and, for us, it was the Warriors, then maybe we could make more of a direct impact.
>
> Some of us knew people who were in AIM ... they brought back a cultural pride that had been missing for so

long, a more positive image for who we were as Indians . . .
AIM activities of the past twenty-five years have helped re-
store the pride and dignity of all native people everywhere
. . . everything they did has had an impact today in all areas,
on native peoples' lives, being proud to be native people
again.

Some of us began to take a look at our own history and traditions and became interested. We wanted to learn more
about our history, to bring our traditions back alive again. So
we asked our fathers and grandfathers to teach us.

This renewed interest in history and cultural heritage (traditions)
contributed to a growing political self-awareness among Mohawks. Further, the strategic insights into the need for pan-Indian
and particular tribal struggles, for centralized and decentralized
but socially networked efforts involving particular issues and land
claims, emerged from analyses of the AIM and its impacts. This
blending of history and cultural heritage with political interests
would ultimately develop into the Mohawk Warrior Movement.

Members of the Mohawk Warrior Movement view themselves as
a domestic army united to maintain the integrity of the Mohawk
nation. In fact, the very concept of "warrior" differs from its common usage in the dominant society, in a symbolic and highly significant manner relevant to the dominant interests. Although the
Mohawk language contains no word that literally translates as "warrior," the Mohawk word "rotiskenrakhete" symbolically means
"warrior." Rotiskenrakhete means those who "carry the responsibility of protecting the origins," or "carry the burden of peace." Although warrior societies did not exist in any formal manner,
throughout Iroquois history there has been a long tradition of the
warrior who defends the community. Thus, today's Mohawk Warrior Movement embodies this image, combining Mohawk historical
traditions with twentieth-century militant strategy. Donnie Martin,
a member of the Kahnawake Warrior Society and part of the
Mohawk Warrior Movement's leadership structure, explains this
self-image:

> . . . it [the Mohawk Warrior Movement] is people who are common to the liberation of the Mohawk people, our territories . . . we have to be free to determine how we govern ourselves, and if this is not the case, then we have a responsibility to liberate that which is oppressed. This is the responsibility of the Warrior Movement.

Mark McComber, who is also a member of the Kahnawake Warrior Society and part of the Mohawk Warrior Movement's leadership structure, adds to this image:

> The Warrior Movement gives us a sense of who we are as Mohawks. But it also gives us a sense of what needs to be done to preserve who we are. We are a movement with a political purpose. That purpose is the continuation of the Mohawk nation as an independent and self-governing nation. And that involves more than cultural preservation. It also involves economic preservation and the right to determine our own economy.
>
> We are able to stand up for who we are because there is a Warrior Movement. Each warrior society has the responsibility to make their community stronger—whether it's protecting jurisdiction, building an economic base, or strengthening a sense of culture. And when each warrior society does that, it makes the whole Mohawk nation stronger.

The Mohawk Warrior Movement is a network of organizations comprised of members from four Mohawk communities: Akwesasne (which straddles the Quebec, Ontario, and New York state borders, thirty-seven miles southwest of Oka and Kanehsatake); Ganienkeh (located in northern New York state twenty miles from the Canadian border); Kahnawake (located in Quebec, Canada, eighteen miles southeast of Oka and Kanehsatake); and Kanehsatake (located within the township of Oka, Quebec). All are part of a single Mohawk nation. The Mohawk Warrior Movement grew out of an institutional base and culture, the Longhouse, and formed from two independent, but interconnected, Mohawk organizations, the Kahnawake Mohawk Society and the Akwesasne Mohawk Society. Michael Thomas, who is a member of the Kahnawake Warrior Society as well as part of the Mohawk Warrior Movement's leadership structure, describes the link between the different warrior societies:

> . . . each of our territories has its own warrior society, but we are linked. We are linked as one Mohawk Warrior Movement to defend all of our territories. We are separate groups, but we come together when it is necessary. Each group has its own leaders and members, but there is a lot of going back and forth between them, helping each other out.

Another movement member, Mark Montour, who is also a member of the Akwesasne Warrior Society, offered the following:

> . . . we act as one. When they act, we act. It's the same. We are part of the same. It's not just the Kahnawake warriors or the Akwesasne warriors. We are also one movement. We are many warrior societies, but we come together as one Warrior Movement, as one Mohawk nation. . . . I have family, friends who are Kahnawake warriors. I am a warrior from Akwesasne. But we are all Mohawk warriors.

This decentralized movement structure of the Mohawk Warrior Movement arose not from rational deduction, vested interests of particular reservations (themselves a result of Euro-Canadian and Euro-American's separation of the Mohawk nation into several locations), nor from strategic opportunity. It arose, as Akwesasne Warrior Society member Loran Thompson explained, because of the impacts of, and as an outgrowth of, the Longhouse and clans, or kinship, networks:

> . . . we are woven together through our clans, through the Longhouse. The Longhouse is our spiritual center, the cultural and political center of the Mohawk community. The community comes together here. It is where our ceremonies take place, where important decisions are made. It is a place where we come to know our history, where we come to know

who we are as Mohawks. It is the place where the warriors are given their responsibilities, it is the place where our responsibilities are taught. Through our clans, through the teachings of the Longhouse, we know who we are, we know what has come before.

Here we see that each Mohawk warrior society is an autonomous movement organization, yet linked to each other in a network-like fashion, forming the larger Mohawk Warrior Movement.

The organization of Mohawk Warrior Movement activity depended on a particular type and level of community organization, endemic to the network-like communal base of the larger Mohawk community. This network contributed to the integration of people from within each, as well as among, the Mohawk territories. Through the Longhouse, the clan-based kinship network structure allowed for cross group or territory relationships, further facilitating the development of warrior societies, and member integration within these organizations and the larger movement. Specifically, the close family and friendship ties and communication provided by these kinship clans encouraged recruitment into the larger Mohawk Warrior Movement. This type of social network facilitated a multilayered sense of commitment and responsibility—to living friends and relatives, as well as ancestors or to historical actors—by movement participants.

Figure 4.1, on the following page, illustrates the nature of this integrated social network structure which helped facilitate Mohawk Warrior Movement member recruitment and protest activity. This social network system operates within the different Mohawk territories as well as between these territories. Specifically, there exists both a vertical social network relationship consisting of the larger Mohawk Warrior Movement and the smaller, more localized, Mohawk warrior society movement organizations (SMOs) and a horizontal social network relationship where the kinship clans permeate all the relationships among the various parts. The idea of vertical and horizontal social networks has been elaborated elsewhere (Tilly and Shorter, 1976) in the context of organizational trade and regional unions.

Figure 4.1. Mohawk Nation Integrated Social Network Structure

Social Movement		WARRIOR MOVEMENT		
		|		
Decentralized SMO's	WARRIOR		SOCIETIES	
	/ \		/ \	
Community	AKWESASNE	GANIENKEH	KAHNAWAKE	KANEHSATAKE
Clans within each cummunity	BEAR CLAN TURTLE WOLF	BEAR CLAN TURTLE WOLF	BEAR CLAN TURTLE WOLF	BEAR CLAN TURTLE WOLF

These social networks are both horizontal and vertical: within Mohawk territories and among Mohawk territories, cross location and cross clan. Additional family networks exist throughout this structure, within territory clan lines and across territory clan lines because of its matriarchal organizational composition.

This particular type of integrated social network structure overcomes the criticisms about and limits of segmented polycentric integrated networks (SPINS). Instead of restricting the coordination of the larger Mohawk Warrior Movement, it actually facilitates coordination. It does so because of the nature of the clan-based kinship network structure, where movement members interact with one another on a regular basis. These individuals have a shared upbringing and expectations. In addition, this particular type of integrated network structure facilitates group cohesion, because, again, individuals come from a similar background and share a common history and experience.

Mobilization and ideology each in part depended on membership in the clan (kinship) network structure. It was within these processes and informal organizations that Mohawks learned who they were and what it meant to be Mohawk, as well as the responsibilities that membership brought with it. Thus, the network was found to facilitate ethnic identity and consciousness formation. The informal organizations created a sense of community, commonality, and solidarity for its members, factors essential to collective identity (Touraine, 1985; Melucci, 1989).

The Mohawk Warrior Movement leaders took advantage of these networks and solicited support based on elements shared by and revered by members of those networks. They recruited participants and resource providers based on common interests, ideas, and obligations arising from memberships in those groups and, constructed a rationale for participation.

Many different groups and institutions play a significant role in Mohawk society—none, however, more so than the Longhouse and the clans. Accordingly, the Longhouse and the clans play a crucial role in the Mohawk Warrior Movement. The cultural and political revival of the Mohawk nation began in the Mohawk territory of Kahnawake, when a group of young Mohawk militants began participating in the Kahnawake Longhouse, learning about Mohawk history and tradition. In 1968, they formed a Mohawk singing society, a group dedicated to reviving the traditional songs of Mohawk culture. It was the first organized group among these Kahnawake militants. In 1972, the Mohawk Singing Society evolved into the Kahnawake Mohawk Warrior Society, becoming an official men's society, or organization of the Kahnawake Longhouse.

During this time, a Mohawk warrior society was also evolving out of the Longhouse at another Mohawk reserve, Akwesasne, in northern New York state. Over the years, Mohawk warrior societies also formed at two other Mohawk territories, Kanehsatake and the newly created Mohawk territory at Ganienkeh. Because Mohawk Warrior Movement members from the different Mohawk territories interact with one another through clan-based kinship networks, members know each other and are able to effectively communicate with one another on both an individual and group level. As a result, although the separate Mohawk warrior societies engage in activity on behalf of their respective Mohawk territories, they also come together, acting on larger issues pertaining to Mohawk nationhood.

Kahnawake Warrior Society member Donnie Martin describes the evolution of the Mohawk Warrior Movement:

> . . . the Movement started out as a cultural movement. It was a movement dedicated to cultural survival. . . . The move-

ment has changed, grown. Now it is a movement dedicated to both cultural and political survival. When we assert our rights to our territory, it's both a cultural statement about our identity as Mohawks, a way of traditional life, and it's a political statement about our identity and right to exist as a nation; our right to jurisdiction.

In another interview, Kahnawake Warrior Society member Mark McComber offered the following:

> ... the Movement has taken on more of a political nature than when it first began. At first, the Movement was a way to bring back our culture's traditions ... for us to [re]gain a sense of our history. Through singing, through the telling of history ... it was a way to [re] gain a sense of who we were, our identity. Then some of us realized that the cultural activities weren't really different, or separate from the political activities that we needed to do in order to preserve the cultural. ... The land, our identity tied up with the land—one might think it's only a cultural thing, but it is also a political thing. Every cultural act the Warrior Movement has engaged in has political ramifications ... our right to nationhood is both a cultural and political right, a right based on history, aboriginal history.

The Mohawk clan kinship system is intricately interwoven with the Longhouse. As is the case for all nations of the Iroquois Confederacy, traditional Mohawk governance is based on matrilineal descent. The social structure within Mohawk society is composed of three clans, or kinship networks: Bear, Turtle, and Wolf. Each Mohawk clan has three women who represent it; they are the clanmothers, who are members of a women's collective or women's society within the Longhouse. Within each clan, a clanmother is collectively selected by the women of her clan. The women for each clan also collectively select two additional women from their respective clans to assist the clanmothers in carrying out their duties and responsibilities. This traditional Mohawk social structure involves hereditary selection of individuals

to represent the Mohawk nation. A similar selection process ap-
plies to Mohawk men. In turn, the clanmothers then select the
Longhouse chiefs for their respective clans to act as the "public"
voice of that clan. Each clan has three chiefs who are ultimately
responsible to their clan and clanmothers. The clanmothers can
remove any chief if he does not act in accordance with the voices
of his clan.

It is important to note that although Mohawk society is a
matrilineal one, power and decision-making rests equally with
both the men and women within Mohawk society. More specifically, although both the men and women have distinct socio-
political functions and responsibilities, political decisions and
other matters of importance affecting the Mohawk nation are
made collectively via consensus of the people.

The Longhouse clan structure is essential to Mohawk society
because it not only defines the cultural and political realms of the
society, but it also shapes society members' collective world view.
Further, it shapes the members' understanding of their collective
duties and responsibilities to the past, present, and future generations of the Mohawk society. The following explanation is offered
by John Cree, spiritual faith keeper for the Longhouse:

> Our clans define who we are as individuals but also who we are
> as families, as a nation and how we all relate to one another.
> . . . It is [within the context of] our clans that Mohawk identity
> informs the spiritual and political thought of our people. It is
> here, in our clans, that our [cultural] values, beliefs, and tradi-
> tions are passed on from generation to generation. . . . Our
> government [structure], laws, language, ceremonies, and other
> [cultural] practices necessary for our national existence are
> maintained here. . . . Without the Longhouse and our clans
> there would be no Mohawk society. It is who we are. Like I said
> before, it defines us.

The Longhouse serves several important functions for the Mohawk Warrior Movement. First, the Longhouse, representing both
the ancestral religion and political life of the Mohawks, creates a

forum in each Mohawk territory for Mohawk Warrior Movement leaders and members where political discussions and decisions take place. Second, as an official men's society, or organization of the Longhouse, the goals and sometimes violent strategies of the Mohawk Warrior Movement become legitimized. Further, recruitment of members into the Mohawk Warrior Movement is facilitated by the clan kinship network that exists within the Longhouse structure.

Francis Boots, a member of the Akwesasne Warrior Society and part of the Mohawk Warrior Movement's leadership structure, explains how the Longhouse clan network functions within the movement:

> It is our Longhouse and clanmothers who support us, who determine our duties and responsibilities to the Mohawk nation—which is to protect the integrity, the sovereignty of the nation. . . . Our war chief is responsible for the warrior's actions, but it is our clanmothers who are responsible for determining if we are to take that action in the first place.

As a result of the factionalized (pro- and anti-warrior), traditional Longhouse government, some of the various Mohawk territories have more than one Longhouse structure operating simultaneously. It is within these territories that the Mohawk Warrior Movement has, in effect, set up a dual Longhouse government structure and a duplicate clan system. The pro-warrior Longhouses have created their own clanmother positions. These clanmothers are chosen from among those women who support the Mohawk Warrior Movement. They in turn select the three pro-warrior Longhouse clan chiefs and war chief.

Loran Thompson, Akwesasne Warrior Society member and part of the Mohawk Warrior Movement's leadership structure, further explains the importance of the (pro-warrior) Longhouse clan network as a key ingredient for the recruitment of movement members:

> . . . because our clans cut across all of our [Mohawk] territories, our members come from a culturally connected group of family . . . who all have the same commitment to Mohawk

sovereignty. Through our clans in our Longhouse we are able to explain to them [other Mohawks] the importance of having . . . and being part of the warrior society.

Thus, this (pro-warrior) Longhouse clan kinship network facilitates member recruitment into the Mohawk Warrior Movement by bringing together the participation of politically similar others.

The process of collective identity formation, in this case ethnic identity, and maintenance is facilitated by participation in the Longhouse. Longhouse participants engage in community activities that are traditionally defined as cultural. These activities include ceremonies or festivals, as well as dances. However, despite their cultural appearance, these activities take on a political significance. Specifically, through these activities, Mohawk history and identity is recalled and transmitted. This practice not only provides one with a sense of who one is within a collectivity (community membership, or identity) but also can encourage and become a vehicle for mobilization of participants into a social movement rooted in that community-based, collective identity. Walter David, Sr., an elder member in the Longhouse, offered this explanation:

It's [the Longhouse] a force for unity . . . the basis of all Mohawk life. Our [Longhouse] ceremonies and dances like the "first fruits of the season," the "first vegetable to ripen," [and] the "Creator's Dance" . . . they bring us together as one. Mohawks have always taken part in these. The younger ones come to know the Mohawk tradition through these, through the Longhouse. . . . The Longhouse teaches them to be Mohawks and what that means to the survival of the Mohawk nation.

Here one sees the importance of the role of the Longhouse for facilitating identity. Culture can be an important means by which collective identity is facilitated. The existence of a Mohawk culture and way of life apart from that of the dominant society, practiced through the Longhouse, facilitates a political interpretation of cultural activities.

The Longhouse facilitates both identity formation and movement mobilization in three ways. First, it creates a forum for political discussion, promoting a heightened awareness (consciousness-raising) of commonality (experiences and interests) that members share. Specifically, members reevaluate and reinterpret their past and current experiences and status, their future opportunities and actions in political terms. This reevaluation and reinterpretation, or consciousness-raising, in turn motivates members to act to change current conditions for the better. Second, through cultural activities or traditions (different ceremonies and festivals and dances) associated with the Longhouse, group membership and solidarity are established and strengthened. And third, embedded within the political culture of the Longhouse is an ideology (nationhood) that supports both the Mohawk Warrior Movement's existence and its strategies of resistance. A discussion of the Mohawk Warrior Movement's ideology will be addressed later in this chapter. However, at this juncture it is important to note that nationhood both reinforces ethnic identity and defines strategies of resistance. In other words, nationhood promotes a sense of community and solidarity, implying that the collectivity embodies a cultural and political identity. By emphasizing historical nationhood as an aboriginal right and defining group boundaries, the Mohawk Warrior Movement asserts Mohawk separatism from the larger, dominant society.

To summarize, ethnic identity, then, is facilitated by participation in the political culture of the Mohawk community, which has its basis in the Longhouse. This identity then, in turn, not only facilitates Mohawk Warrior Movement mobilization but also shapes the movement's goals and strategies of resistance, much like "cultural feminism" (Ferree & Hess, 1985; Whittier & Taylor, 1989).

THE DRIVING FORCE BEHIND THE MOVEMENT

Because ideologies are socially constructed sets of personal beliefs that interpret experiences and guide political actions (Leibich, 1983:225), it is important that one understand the ideology that motivates political actions of Mohawk Warrior Movement members. The driving force behind the movement is an ideology of nationalism, or Mohawk sovereignty. It is an ideology that is embraced by every Mohawk territory, symbolized by their flying of the Mohawk Warrior Movement's red-and-yellow flag (a silhouette of a warrior with a traditional Iroquois scalp lock and a single feather against a red-and-yellow background). Since 1973, the Mohawk Warrior Movement has raised this flag in every act of protest in which its members have engaged. During the Mohawk-Oka crisis in 1990, it became a symbol of Mohawk nationalism and was raised defiantly over the barricades at Kanehsatake and Kahnawake.

To understand the Mohawk Warrior Movement's ideology, one must recognize that it arises from a responsibility to a particular historical concept of nationhood. Mohawk Warrior Movement ideology must be understood within the context of members' resolve to practice their own ways of thinking and act consistent with those nationalist beliefs. For example, Mohawk Warrior Movement members argue that the Mohawk right to nationhood and self-determination is an inherent right and that aboriginal sovereignty has existed since "time immemorial." This is explained by Mohawk Warrior Movement leader Allan Delaronde:

> . . . first let me say that the only power that exists for any people, whether it is Mohawks, or any nation, lies in the decision of the people to determine who they are and to assert their nationhood. . . . We, as Mohawks, must define our own identity. Our power comes from within . . . our strength as Mohawks comes from our identity. Nationhood is the central issue here.
>
> Our identity comes from nationhood. We have a responsibility to defend that, defend our right to exist as a nation, to exist as Mohawks. . . . It is important for all Mohawks to understand that we are being subjected to a process that has as its primary purpose the denial of our right to nationhood and, with that, the removal of our identity as Mohawk people, as native people. Our right to nationhood, to exist as the Mohawk nation is a historical right. . . .

Sovereignty, it is a difficult word to define. It is very much like an inherent quality. It is absolute . . . it is the absolute power of a people to govern themselves. It comes before nationhood because it is an aboriginal right. That right has existed long before their [Canadian] government and their laws. It comes from within a people, it is aboriginal, and aboriginal sovereignty cannot be given to one group by another. . . . I think you can understand now what, as you call it, motivates the movement.

The Mohawk Warrior Movement has an ideology that espouses violence within a specific context. Specifically, members embrace violent self-defense in pursuit of its nationalist political and economic agenda. Diane Lazore, a high-ranking female member of the Mohawk Warrior Movement from Akwesasne, offered the following:

. . . our goal is to protect the interests of the Mohawk nation. If we want to be able to exercise greater control over our own lives and destiny as a people, as a nation, then we must develop strategies that will see to that goal. It seems of late that these strategies have had to be strategies of violence. They [the Canadian government] understand violence very well . . . we have accomplished many things with violence. Some of us prefer the route of peaceful lobbying and negotiations, and we have tried that route on many occasions . . . but we are also not adverse to using militant tactics, if that's what it takes to accomplish our objective.

We can no longer afford to sit around and wait until the federal government decides when it is the appropriate time to give us greater control. We must take control ourselves, and we must take control now. We want the opportunity to determine what happens in our own communities and, unfortunately, they [the federal government] only listen when we use force. Our objective—to protect Mohawk interests—has always been the same. It's our methods that have changed, [and they have changed] because they have had to.

Minnie Garrow, another member in the armed movement from Akwesasne, justifies the use of violence, not as an end in itself but in response to the failure of other strategies:

> . . . we have tried many times to preserve aboriginal sovereignty through negotiations. But there are times, many times, when these good intentions fall on deaf ears. We have gone to their [Canadian and United States] courts, their systems of justice. We have come to know that this does not work . . . we will never be able to achieve legal recognition of Mohawk nationhood through negotiation. We have come to recognize that direct action is our most potent political weapon . . . violence or the threat [of violence] seems to be understood. . . . It has fallen upon the warriors . . . the responsibility to fight this battle.

Dale Dion, a member of the movement from Kahnawake, echoes the self-protective and strategic (almost pragmatic) use of violent actions and tactics. And, she has pointed out its implications on self- and collective identity:

> There are times when you have to use violence, especially when the very core of your existence is being threatened. We can not allow the future of the Mohawk nation to be decided by outsiders . . . the issue of Mohawk nationhood is not a debatable issue, just as our aboriginal right to land is not. Violence is respected . . . they listen . . . they fear violence. Violence has given us bargaining power. It seems that when we [the Warrior Movement] use violence then we are a threat . . . then we are taken seriously . . . then they say, well let's talk about the issues. We can do a lot to threaten, to make them fear, to make them listen. We demonstrated this at Oka . . . we showed our strength . . . strength through violence . . . we paralyzed them. We took control of the Mercier [bridge] . . . we disrupted people's lives . . . they could not drive to work. When you hurt them at their wallet, people begin to listen. They [the white man] have come to know this, and if

they have not yet learned then they will . . . the time for talk-
ing is over. . . . It's time for action.

The shared belief in the value of nationhood became the reso-
nating ideological framework for the Mohawk Warrior Movement
in its mobilization of participant support. The movement succeeded in generating participant support because of its ability to
link its goals as a movement with an ideological perspective
attractive to and reflective of the culture and identity of its
constituency.

The value of nationhood, or aboriginal sovereignty, coupled
with an already networked and organized constituency, provided
the ideological rationale for reasserting aboriginal rights through
protest activity. As Jenkins (1983) observed on recruitment strategies, the ability of the Mohawk Warrior Movement to successfully forge ahead depended on "campaigns centered around
purposive and solidary incentives, focusing on preexisting groups"
(p. 538). In this case, they created incentives for other Mohawks
through the clan kinship network and different Mohawk Warrior
societies. The Mohawk Warrior Movement's ability to recruit
members depended on providing a culturally based ideology to
mobilize ideological commitments held by members of already existing groups (Ferree & Miller, 1985).

At its heart, this ideology of nationalism is founded on the
Great Law of Peace, or the Constitution of the Iroquois Confederacy (Hall, 1987). This religious doctrine combines rules of spiritual and political action. Joe David, a member of the Kanehsatake
Warrior Society, explains:

> . . . our responsibility as warriors has been given to us by the
> Great Law. It teaches us that we have a responsibility to
> help defend the Mohawk people. As Mohawks and as war-
> riors, it is our responsibility to stand up for our rights, to de-
> fend those rights, to protect our territory. Warriors have a
> responsibility to preserve Mohawk sovereignty, to protect
> Mohawk nationhood.

Several of the doctrine's 117 articles (known as Wampums) specifically refer to the role and responsibilities of the Longhouse war chief and the warriors, as well as endorse the use of violence (warfare) as a "legitimate" strategy in order to protect the Iroquois Confederacy from outside aggressors. For example, Wampum 37 specifies that one of the responsibilities of the Longhouse war chief is "to take up arms" to defend the territory; Wampum 91 authorizes the warriors to "resist invasion" of territory by declaring a war; and Wampum 80 authorizes warfare against any foreign nation that threatens the existence of the Iroquois Confederacy (Hall, 1987; York & Pindera, 1991). It is important to note here that such references within the Great Law of Peace would thus seem to indicate and link the historical (and contemporary) significance and important role of the warrior societies (movement) within Mohawk culture. The leaders of the Mohawk Warrior Movement have incorporated elements of the Great Law of Peace into their political ideology. Consistent with the doctrine, members of the Mohawk Warrior Movement believe in the use of violence (warfare) to maintain the integrity of Mohawk nationhood. Thus, within their own legal and spiritual framework, the warriors are more akin to a national guard or state militia than any criminal or terrorist group. And, their goals are the antithesis of criminals and terrorists.

Members of the Mohawk Warrior Movement have a very definite conception of what their ideology of nationalism means to them, or rather what form they would like to see Mohawk nationhood, or sovereignty, take. Francis Boots, a Mohawk Warrior Movement leader, defines this concept:

> We [the Mohawk Warrior Movement] have always stood firm that as a sovereign nation the jurisdictional authority of any foreign government is rejected within all of the Mohawk territories . . . and if they try to impose their laws on any of our territories, it is our responsibility as a nation to defend our territory by our law . . . it is our responsibility as warriors to defend Mohawk territory from outside aggressors.

This ideology of nationalism you asked me about, it involves the continuation of the Mohawk nation, plain and simple. And you must understand, this involves much more than just cultural survival. It also means economic survival, that's the bottom line. It [nationhood] is our right to decide for ourselves what types of jobs we will make for our territories. By building an economic base, we guarantee the survival of the Mohawk nation, culturally and politically. . . . It [nationhood] means [our] complete jurisdiction over our territory . . . [over our] political and economic interests.

It is important to note at this juncture that the legitimacy of the Mohawk Warrior Movement rests on the status initially granted by the Kahnawake Longhouse. In 1972, the chiefs of the three Mohawk clans officially granted the Kahnawake Warrior Society legitimate status as a men's society of the Kahnawake Longhouse. Louis Hall, a key figure in the revival of the warrior society tradition, considered the ideological founder of the Mohawk Warrior Movement by its members, was a council member in the Kahnawake Longhouse who in 1972 helped authorize the sanctioning of the Warrior Society as an official organization of the Kahnawake Longhouse. He became one of the early leaders of the Mohawk Warrior Movement and, in 1979, wrote the warrior's handbook *Rebuilding the Iroquois Confederacy*. However, it is equally important to note here that the Mohawk Warrior Movement's continued legitimacy rests only with the pro-warrior Longhouses (Mohawk Nation Councils) within the Mohawk territories of Kahnawake and Ganienkeh and with pro-warrior factions within the Longhouses of Akwesasne and Kanehsatake. The Mohawk Warrior Movement does not have universal legitimacy within the Mohawk nation or the Iroquois Confederacy. Specifically, none of the three governing bodies of Akwesasne, the Mohawk Nation Council, the St. Regis Tribal Council, the Mohawk Council of Akwesasne, the Kanehsatake Band Council, or the Iroquois Grand Council have granted the Mohawk Warrior Movement legitimate status.

The factional situation within the various territories of the Mohawk nation warrants further explanation. Political cleavages within these various Mohawk territories are rooted in the development and institutionalization of colonial policies and practices, by both the Canadian and American governments. For example, the Indian Advancement Act, an 1885 amendment to the Indian Act in Canada, was created to intensify political cleavages within the Mohawk territories by imposing foreign political systems (forms of government) known as "Elected Band Councils" as replacements for the traditional Longhouse government (Miller, 1991). The Band Council is elected by members of the reservation community and does not follow the Great Law of Peace, or the Constitution of the Iroquois Confederacy. Because the Band Council receives financial support from the federal government, it is accountable to the Department of Indian Affairs and Northern Development (DIAND). The establishment of such colonial political institutions served to destabilize and depoliticize the traditional government structure of the Longhouse, a strategy devised to deny the political existence and power of the Mohawk traditional government system.

Members of the Longhouse and, as such, of the Mohawk Warrior Movement, openly reject the Canadian government-sanctioned, elected Band Council. Instead, these men and women favor and openly practice the government of the Great Law of Peace, or the Constitution of the Iroquois Confederacy. Allen Gabriel, a member of the Longhouse who took part in the occupation of "The Pines," explained:

> We reject white-sponsored Mohawk government . . . we do not recognize the [Band] Council, and we do not participate in their elections. They are not the true voice of the Mohawk people . . . they are not the traditional voice. They are the government's puppets. They are put into power by the Canadian government . . . financed by the government to set up a puppet Band Council government. It keeps their law over our land . . . so that they can keep their foot around our neck . . .

making us more dependent on their ways. . . . We follow Mohawk traditional religion. That's the real government, the real voice of the Mohawk people.

Although many Mohawks support the Mohawk Warrior Movement, there are those, including other members of the Iroquois Confederacy, who do not. These critics of the Mohawk Warrior Movement consider its members to be a violent gang of criminals who advocate terrorism. Clearly, in terms of self-perception and avowed goals, Mohawk Warrior Movement members do not portray or recognize themselves as such. Yet, they have many critics, and some of these critics are themselves members of the Longhouse. To understand the underpinnings of this factionalized debate over the legitimacy of the Mohawk Warrior Movement, one needs to understand the nature of Iroquois government.

There are two forms of governing structures that exist and operate simultaneously within Mohawk society. First is the traditional hereditary government structure of the Iroquois Confederacy, which pre-dates European contact. This traditional hereditary government structure, the Iroquois Grand Council located at Onondaga, New York, and its counterpart, the Iroquois Grand Council, located at Grand River, Ontario, serve as the Confederacy's executive governing body. They oversee the following six Nation Councils: Mohawk (called the Kahnawake Longhouse at Kahnawake), Oneida, Onondaga, Tuscarora, Cayuga, and Seneca, based on the Great Law of Peace. This governing structure is not recognized by the governments of Canada or the United States.

Second is the nontraditional elected reservation governing structure consisting of the St. Regis Tribal Council at Akwesasne, (United States), established in 1802, and its counterpart, the Mohawk Council of Akwesasne (Quebec and Ontario, Canada), established in 1899, the Kahnawake Mohawk Band Council, and the Kanehsatake Band Council. They were created and are recognized by both the governments of Canada and the United States. Elections for the position of grand chief and sub-chiefs are held every three years. It is important to note that although the governments of both Canada and the United States currently fail to recognize the legitimacy of the traditional hereditary Nation Councils, all treaties that were signed between these two nations and the Mohawk Nation before 1800 were signed with the Mohawk Nation Council.

At the center of the Mohawk Warrior Movement legitimacy debate are two interpretations of Iroquois history, which ironically involve two factions (a militant faction associated with supporting the Mohawk Warrior Movement and another faction that opposes the movement) of the traditional hereditary governing structure of the Iroquois Confederacy. These factions are at odds with one another over the interpretation of the Great Law of Peace, also known as the Constitution of the Iroquois Confederacy. However, a third faction, the nontraditional elected reservation governing structure, is also involved in the debate concerning the legitimacy of the Mohawk Warrior Movement.

The two Longhouse factions differ in their interpretations of the Great Law of Peace's authorization of the use of violence as a necessary and legitimate strategy to defend sovereign Mohawk territory. The Mohawk Warrior Movement's interpretation of the Iroquois Great Law of Peace is very similar to the version documented by anthropologist Arthur C. Parker (1916). One of the earliest-known translations of the Great Law of Peace, it is essentially the version followed by the Longhouse at Kahnawake and Ganienkeh, as well as by pro-warrior factions within the Longhouses at Akwesasne and Kanehsatake. The interpretation of the Great Law of Peace, which is espoused by the Mohawk Warrior Movement and distributed by the pro-warrior Mohawk Nation Office at Kahnawake, is synthesized by Louis Hall, the movement's ideological leader.

The faction of the Longhouse that opposes the Mohawk Warrior Movement follows the oral version of the Great Law of Peace that is heavily influenced by the pacifist teachings of Handsome Lake. This faction of the Longhouse supports, and is supported by, the Iroquois Grand Council. Louis Hall argues that the Iroquois Grand Council's interpretation of the Great Law of Peace is illegitimate because it follows some of the concepts of the Code of Handsome Lake. The Code of Handsome Lake combines aspects of Christian religion with native traditions. As such, the members of the Mohawk Warrior Movement argue that their interpretation of the Great Law of Peace is the correct one because it is based on a non-Christian spiritual cosmology, and thus they are the legitimate representatives of the Mohawk nation.

Note that it was Handsome Lake who borrowed many of the Great Law of Peace's concepts for his Code of Handsome Lake and not vice versa. Nevertheless, Hall criticizes the Iroquois Grand Council because it chooses to follow a peace-oriented path of teachings. Hall and the Mohawk Warrior Movement stress the use of direct action that can often result in armed conflict.

The split between the two factions of the Longhouse is ultimately a disagreement over tactics, as Mohawk Warrior Movement leaders have adapted the teachings of the Great Law of Peace to contemporary political and legal, as well as economic, conditions. Both sides are committed to Mohawk nationhood and economic self-determination, but they are divided over the methods by which to secure them. Supporters of the Iroquois Grand Council system of government maintain that the Mohawk Warrior Movement's (neo-traditionalist) interpretation of the Great Law of Peace is a bastardization of traditional Longhouse teachings. Additionally, the Iroquois Grand Council denounced members of the Mohawk Warrior Movement for using an illegitimate interpretation of history for the benefit of furthering their own personal and collective economic and political interests (Statement of Iroquois Grand Council, Onondaga, New York, December 23, 1989).

Further, there are those opponents who maintain that Mohawk tradition does not authorize the role of the warriors akin to that of the movement's self-image. Although the Mohawk traditional form of government does include the position of a war chief within its social structure, opponents of the Mohawk Warrior Movement contend that there does not exist any paramilitary-type men's society within Mohawk tradition.

When questioned about the responsibility of leadership and decision-making within the Mohawk Warrior Movement, Francis Boots, Akwesasne Warrior Society member and a movement spokesman, offered the following:

> . . . although one person is responsible for coordinating ac-
> tivities and this is the war chief of the Longhouse, no one
> person has the power to make military or political decisions
> outright. . . . The warriors are a society in the Longhouse,
> and the war chief of the Longhouse coordinates activities for
> the warrior society. Each warrior society has its own leaders
> in place. There is the war chief, and there are also three assis-
> tant war chiefs who represent the three different clans: Bear,
> Turtle, and Wolf. This is the chain of command that all
> members must adhere to. . . . If it is an activity that requires
> the attention of the war chief and assistants from all the war-
> rior societies, then we make decisions by consensus among all
> the Longhouse war chiefs and assistants.

Even with regard to military-type decision-making within the Mohawk Warrior Movement, Mohawk women again exercise a great deal of power in determining military policy. As in the past, the decision to exercise military-type action is an issue that is dis-cussed and debated by both the Mohawk men and women. Spe-cifically, after the Longhouse chiefs have decided on military action, they are required to bring this decision before the women of their respective clans, upon which the women of all three clans are required to reach a consensus. If such a consensus is in agree-ment with the men's decision, the subsequent military action is then the responsibility of the Longhouse war chief and the warrior society. The Mohawk warrior societies, which together comprise the Mohawk Warrior Movement, then operate under the jurisdic-tion of the war chiefs of their respected Mohawk territories. Further, although what has been described above is a map of the organizational leadership, there exists other leader-type individu-als who serve as public spokespersons for the movement. Most of these individuals form a core of Mohawk intellectuals. Having graduated from Canadian and U.S. universities, these leaders have brought to the movement a repertoire of "legitimate" as well as "illegitimate" strategies.

SUMMARY

As a number of social movement theorists have argued, social protest is an activity that depends, in part, on mobilizing or constructing social networks and "cultures of solidarity" (Fantasia, 1988; Klandermans & Oegema, 1987; McAdam, 1988; Morris, 1984; Scott, 1990; Snow, Zurcher, & Ekland-Olson, 1980). These social networks can exist within communities as well as between communities with shared similar interests. When one examines Mohawk Warrior Movement participation, one finds that movement recruitment and protest activity was facilitated, in part, by the existence of segmented, polycentric, integrated (social or community) networks (SPINS, cf. Gerlach, 1983; Gerlach & Hine, 1970). This type of movement structure is composed of localized groups that are independent but can come together through a networked relationship to form a larger movement. However, scholars of social movements have criticized this type of movement structure, arguing that it restricts the coordination of the larger movement and that cohesion is difficult to maintain (Dwyer, 1983; McAdam, 1982). But the clan-based kinship network structure of the Mohawk Warrior Movement ameliorates these problems.

Specifically, the existence of an integrated social network system and the extent of member integration within these networks were instrumental in the formation of the Mohawk Warrior Movement. The clan-based kinship network (horizontal network system) is the site from which the most fundamental group processes emerge. The clan-based kinship network that exists within and among the separate Mohawk territories provides the common thread by which individuals interact with one another, sharing common experiences and interests. These clan-based kinship networks contributed to the initial process of social movement group formation. In particular, history was used as a resource for mobilization facilitation and identity formation. The clans, which transmit a sense of history, teach Mohawks a sense of who they are, allowing them to become self-consciously aware. In addition, through prior integration in these kinship networks, Mohawk Warrior Movement leaders have been able to recruit participants.

The Longhouse serves many functions for the Mohawk Warrior Movement. It provides a place where the different Mohawk warrior societies come together to coordinate their sense of purpose, to mobilize movement capacity in pursuit of certain goals. It is the Longhouse that sanctions the Mohawk Warrior Movement and its various Mohawk warrior societies (movement organizations), allowing them to exist as formal organizations. In other words, the Longhouse provides legitimacy to the existence of the Mohawk Warrior Movement by sanctioning it as an official organization. The Longhouse sponsorship becomes a resource because it provides a legitimized type of domestic army, rather than just a group of "terrorists," for the Mohawk nation.

The network of different Mohawk warrior societies further enhanced the processes of group formation: consciousness of identity and development of group solidarity. It is here that movement members began to develop a politicized collective identity, merging cultural heritage with political interests. This men's society of the Longhouse evolved into separate, yet linked, Mohawk warrior societies that are situated within the larger Mohawk Warrior Movement. Participation in the Mohawk Warrior Movement reflects the networked relations and coalitions among the different Mohawk warrior societies.

The different Mohawk warrior societies (network of territory organizations, or vertical network system) further enhanced the processes of group formation, identity and consciousness formation, and group solidarity. Clearly, it was found that these networks, in conjunction with participation in the Longhouse, the spiritual and political center of traditional Mohawk life, create a forum within the territory where political discussions and decisions occur. This in turn creates a sense of community and solidarity. By providing interaction with similar others, these social networks facilitate and strengthen the formation of ethnic identity and consciousness, as well as foster a sense of solidarity and responsibility within members. This in turn motivates them to participate in Mohawk Warrior Movement activity. Therefore, filial ties (networks) contribute to a shared sense of grievances and movement development and member participation. Thus, these networks (movement organizations) foster a larger politicized collective (ethnic) identity and consciousness.

5

The Mobilization of
Mohawk Warrior Militancy

The Mohawk Warrior Movement's efforts during the Mohawk-Oka conflict at Kanehsatake and Kahnawake in 1990 did not occur in isolation. Rather, its actions were deeply rooted in what has come to be known as Mohawk protest tradition. Over the years, the Mohawk Warrior Movement has engaged in various protest activities. Mobilization first occurred in the late '60s and early '70s, as members of the Mohawk Warrior Movement asserted their aboriginal right to sovereignty with increasing effectiveness. Treaty rights were tested, territory and jurisdiction were defended, and expropriated lands were reclaimed. It was during this time that the Mohawk Warrior Movement began engaging in direct action.

The earliest protest activities engaged in by members of the Mohawk Warrior Movement were relatively peaceful, nonviolent confrontations. In 1968, a group of Mohawks seized the Seaway International Bridge, which crosses the Akwesasne Reserve, connecting parts of the reserve in Canada and the United States on Cornwall Island (*Malone Evening Telegram*, 1968). Members were protesting Canada's enforcement of a customs tax on goods carried across the international border by Mohawks (York & Pindera,

1991). Because the Akwesasne Mohawk reserve straddles the United States and Canadian borders, the central issue behind the bridge blockade was the recognition of Mohawk nationhood. Herbert Bush, Akwesasne Warrior Society member, explains:

> . . . they wanted to set the law for us. No outside government has the right to impose its laws on another nation. Only Mohawk government can say to its members what rules and laws they should follow. We do not recognize this border that they claim. Our nation is a single nation, the Mohawk nation, not two separate nations, not the American and the Canadian Mohawk nation, one whole Mohawk nation. How can you charge customs [duties] for goods that you are purchasing within your own nation. . . .

In 1970, with the help of members from the Kahnawake Mohawk Warrior Society, the Akwesasne Mohawk Warrior Society reclaimed two islands (Stanley Island and Loon Island) of traditional Mohawk territory in the St. Lawrence River (*Malone Evening Telegram*, 1970).

As the Mohawk Warrior Movement became a political force to contend with, they were asked to help other Iroquois nations. During 1971, members of the Mohawk Warrior Movement joined forces with Longhouse activists from the Onondaga Nation, south of Syracuse in New York state, to disrupt the expansion construction of Highway 81, an interstate route that passes through the Onondaga reservation (*Syracuse Post Standard*, 1971a). The issue motivating this protest was the expropriation of Iroquois land. Members of the Mohawk Warrior Movement occupied the construction site for several weeks. As a result, several confrontations erupted between the New York State Police and protesters (*Syracuse Post Standard*, 1971b). An agreement was finally reached between the state of New York and the Onondaga nation, at which time members of the Mohawk Warrior Movement permitted construction to resume. That agreement provided monetary compensation to the Onondagas for the land they would lose because of the expansion construction of Highway 81.

In 1973, members of the Mohawk Warrior Movement took the issue of Mohawk nationhood to a new level as they initiated and enforced an eviction campaign. The campaign resulted when members of the Mohawk Warrior Movement discovered that a non-Mohawk family had been granted permission from the local government to purchase and build a house on a parcel of land on the Kahnawake reserve (*Montreal Gazette*, 1973a). Because of a severe shortage of land for housing in Kahnawake, many Mohawks were angered by the presence of non-native residents on the reserve (York & Pindera, 1991). Members of the Mohawk Warrior Movement felt it was their duty to send out eviction notices to all non-natives who were living on the reserve.

Although most of the non-native residents agreed to leave Kahnawake, there were a few who refused to exit. As a result, members of the Mohawk Warrior Movement engaged in physical eviction practices, taking over residents' houses and occupying them (*Montreal Gazette*, 1973b). The Surete du Quebec (SQ, the Quebec provincial police) were called to Kahnawake by the non-native residents who were forcibly evicted by members of the Mohawk Warrior Movement (ibid.) A confrontation ensued between the Quebec police and members of the Mohawk Warrior Movement. Several movement members were arrested for breaking and entering and were taken to a local police station in neighboring Chateauguay, Quebec (ibid.) Additional officers from the provincial police force were sent to Kahnawake to patrol the reserve. Believing that the Quebec police had no jurisdiction on Mohawk territory, further confrontations ensued, erupting into a riot (York & Pindera, 1991). Not willing to risk reverberations across native Canada, the officers withdrew.

In the spring of 1974, leaders of the Mohawk Warrior Movement set in motion a plan to repossess 612 acres of traditional Mohawk territory in the Adirondack Mountains in northern New York state (Landsman, 1988). The area, Moss Lake, was a state-owned, abandoned Girl Scout camp. The Mohawks (re) named the territory Ganienkeh, "Land of the Flint," the traditional name for Mohawk land (Campbell, 1985; Landsman, 1988). The (re) occupation turned into an armed conflict between the warriors and the local residents and New York State Police.

Eventually, New York state officials entered into negotiations with the Mohawks, and in 1977 an agreement was reached (Landsman, 1988). The Mohawks agreed to leave the Moss Lake area in exchange for a 698-acre site in Clinton County, near the town of Altona, just south of the Canadian border. This new site was also named Ganienkeh. Here, too, one sees another important precedent that will affect the events of the 1990 Mohawk-Oka conflict. The New York state government, in response to an armed uprising regarding native land claims, created a definable Mohawk territory. This claim had substantially less legal standing than did the Kanehsatake claim. Given the historical findings regarding Kahnawake and the concessions at Ganienkeh, the Canadian government's position on the Kanehsatake land claims appeared more capricious, prejudicial, and illegitimate.

Because of a lack of money to help finance the Mohawk Warrior Movement's political agenda, the movement was relatively quiet for several years, until confrontations over Mohawk Warrior Movement economy erupted in the early 1980s. The Mohawk Warrior Movement believed that lucrative business enterprises were needed to help finance the Mohawk nation and its defense (the nation's defense being the Mohawk Warrior Movement). Focusing on the need for Mohawk nation enterprises, Akwesasne Warrior Society member Gordon Lazore explains how Mohawks must begin to achieve economic self-sufficiency:

> . . . how can we take control of our communities when so many of us are dependent on the federal government for economic assistance. We cannot be politically independent if we are economically dependent. We must first become economically independent before we can be politically independent. . . . Part of the warrior's responsibility to the nation is to develop that economic independence.
>
> For us to solve our problems of dependency we must first be able to rely on a stable economy within the Mohawk community. The casinos allow that; they allow us to build that stable

economy. We can expand our economy with the casino money. By pumping money into the community we reduce our dependence on the federal government. Mohawk political independence and survival is dependent on Mohawk economic independence.

In another interview, Rowena General, who is also a member of the Akwesasne Warrior Society, offered the following:

Akwesasne, Kahnawake, Kanehsatake are part of a single Mohawk nation. And every nation needs money to keep it strong, to provide jobs for its people. They [the government] have taken away our strength, our ability to provide for ourselves. The cigarettes and casinos are our form of [gaining] money, of [securing] jobs for our people. This is something we have developed on our own. No one is giving it to us. It is not just for the warriors, it is for Mohawk people, the Mohawk nation.

The tax-free cigarette industry was introduced into the Mohawk territories of Akwesasne and Kahnawake in 1980. Many of the cigarette entrepreneurs were either members of the Mohawk Warrior Movement itself or supporters of the movement. Although Canadian and U.S. law dictates that untaxed cigarettes were to be sold only to indigenous peoples living on the reservation, Mohawk cigarette entrepreneurs have extended this right to all customers. This practice has resulted in non-native residents of neighboring communities comprising the principal clientele for the cigarette dealers. Because the Mohawks can sell cigarettes without attaching a tax, non-natives can purchase the product at a significantly lower price than if they bought the same product at their local store. Canadians avoided a luxury tax placed on tobacco products, and Americans avoided a state sales tax.

This exemption from sales taxation is a well-established right for Mohawks living on the reservation. As a result of the Jay Treaty of 1793 between Great Britian and the United States, Mohawks are guaranteed the right to cross tax-free, with personal goods, the border between the two countries. Various Mohawks have used this guaranteed treaty right to divert untaxed Canadian cigarettes bound for the United States back into Canada, in order to sell them in the Mohawk territory of Kahnawake where they are not subject to taxation under Canadian law. Specifically, to escape the Canadian government's luxury tax, cigarettes are shipped into the United States as export products. Using the proximity and convenience of the border at Akwesasne, they are then shipped to the Mohawk reserve of Kahnawake in Quebec, Canada. The untaxed cigarettes can then be purchased at smoke shops on the Kahnawake reserve.

Both the Canadian provincial and U.S. state governments have branded this attempt by Mohawks, that of building a profitable economic industry, as an illegal enterprise. Both the Canadian provincial and U.S. state governments claim they have lost millions of dollars a year in tax revenues. In Canada, a carton of cigarettes costs the wholesaler $9 before the Canadian government adds its $21 luxury tax, bringing the retail cost for a carton of cigarettes to $30. The Mohawks undercut the off-reservation price of cigarettes by selling a carton of cigarettes for $12, making a $3 profit on each carton. The government of Canada allows its citizens to purchase and take back over the border two cartons of cigarettes duty- (tax-) free. Additionally, the Iroquois Grand Council also opposes the cigarette trade, arguing that such an economic industry violates the Jay Treaty by exploiting tax-free status in order to achieve personal profit. This assertive interpretation also contradicts the Mohawk Warrior Movement's claim that such an economic industry benefits the Mohawk nation collective (as members of the Mohawk Warrior Movement so often proclaimed that their involvement in such economic activity was doing).

The tax-free cigarette industry has proved to be very profitable for the pro-warrior Longhouse and the Mohawk Warrior Movement itself. In a profit-sharing arrangement, the cigarette entrepreneurs contribute a percentage of their profits to the Longhouse. For example, York and Pindera (1991) state that in Kahnawake

> some retailers gave seventy cents to the Longhouse for every carton of cigarettes they sold. Almost half of this percentage

went to the Warrior Society. According to internal Long-house documents, the Warriors were given a total of about $350,000 in payments by cigarette retailers over [a period of] two years. (p. 185)

The collective Mohawk territory of Kahnawake has benefitted from the tax-free cigarette as well. At its most profitable peak in 1990, the tax-free cigarette industry contributed $75 million to the local Kahnawake economy. According to York and Pindera (1991),

> the cigarette donations financed a wide range of community projects: more than $12,000 in medical equipment for the Kahnawake hospital . . . a business fund which gave interest-free loans of up to $5,000 each to Mohawk entrepreneurs, about $30,000 in Mohawk language tapes and books, funding for the construction of a new Longhouse, a Mohawk language immersion program for pre-school children, an anti-pollution program, and an alcohol and drug counselling program. (p. 130)

The gaming industry was introduced into the Mohawk territory of Akwesasne in 1983 when the first bingo hall was established. Again, non-native residents of neighboring communities were the principal clientele. Various members of the Mohawk Warrior Movement and other Mohawks who engaged in the cigarette trade formed the core of the pro-gambling faction. Some members of the Mohawk Warrior Movement were themselves owners, co-owners, and/or managers of the gaming establishments, while other members of the movement provided the armed security for those establishments. Profits gained from the cigarette trade funded the start-up costs for the gambling establishemnts. Additionally, a member of the Akwesasne Mohawk Warrior Society, who asked not to be identified, revealed that the various Mohawk warrior societies and the Mohawk Warrior Movement itself has been funded by the cigarette and gambling trade which has been established in various Mohawk territories. Both the cigarette and bingo economy have been operating in the Mohawk territories of Akwesasne, Ganienkeh, and Kahnawake, while high-stakes gambling has been operating in Akwesasne. Kanehsatake operated a small-scale bingo hall, however, he would not reveal the specifics as to how the gaming profits reached the Mohawk Warrior Movement.

When the first bingo hall opened in the Mohawk territory of Akwesasne in 1983, it was sanctioned by the St. Regis Tribal Council. As an authorized franchise of the Council, it was obligated to provide 49 percent of the establishment's profits to the St. Regis Tribal Council. It would appear that when gambling began, the St. Regis Tribal Council governing structure favored it, as it was contributing to their coffers. Note that the St. Regis Tribal Council only voiced its opposition to gambling after the owner of the bingo establishment did not follow through on his scheduled profit payments. Thus, it appears it is not gambling per se that is the problem for elected tribal officials, but rather individually owned (and individually profiting) gaming establishments. Mohawk government controlled and regulated gaming establishments that contribute some amount of their profits to the government budget for community projects and development seem to be subject to much less of a conflict.

However, the Mohawk Nation Council contends that gambling is not an appropriate way to build a viable community economy. Therefore, it has never supported high-stakes bingo and other forms of commercial gambling. They argue that ". . . high-stakes commercial gambling, uncontrolled and unregulated, has a destructive influence on our people; it leads to political and cultural destruction" (Mohawk Nation Council press release, July 24, 1989). Harold Tarbell, the anti-gambling Chief of the St. Regis Tribal Council, also voiced his opposition to gambling, arguing that ". . . illegal casinos, cigarette smuggling . . . [were] all done in the name of Mohawk sovereignty, but [were really] done for personal advantage" (*Press Republican*, Plattsburgh, NY, May 12, 1990). Both of these statements seem to imply that the personal business interests of individual members of the Mohawk Warrior Movement hide behind the smokescreen of the aboriginal sovereign right of economic self-determination.

The internal conflict within the Mohawk nation surrounding the issue of gambling involves three principal factions. These factions consist of the traditional hereditary Mohawk Nation Council; the state-sanctioned, elected St. Regis Tribal Council and its Canadian counterpart, the Mohawk Council of Akwesasne (all of which are anti-gambling); and the Mohawk Warrior Movement and its pro-warrior and pro-gambling constituents. For the Mohawk Nation Council the conflict revolves around the corruption of Mohawk culture; for the St. Regis Tribal Council it revolves around control and regulation of the gaming establishments and their profits; and for the Mohawk Warrior Movement it revolves around the issue of sovereignty and economic self-determination.

The conflict over gambling between the anti-gambling and pro-gambling factions was also taking place in the Canadian Mohawk territories of Kanehsatake and Kahnawake. Political cleavages developed as Mohawks who favored bingo clashed with those Mohawks who supported the Elected Band Council's and Canada's federal government policy against gambling. This issue of economic self-determination has ignited a piggyback conflict revolving around individual sovereignty rights versus the Mohawk nation's collective sovereignty rights.

Stated very succinctly in *Akwesasne Notes*, a national indigenous newspaper housed in the Mohawk territory of Akwesasne, the fundamental issues that shape the Mohawk nation's internal conflict over gambling are threefold: "Whether the people want commercial gambling on their land and, if so, whether it ought to be operated privately or as a tribal enterprise, and should casino gambling be allowed or just high-stakes bingo" (early summer 1990). Those who favor gambling as a form of economic development argue that the reservations need the self-sustaining jobs that the bingo halls and casinos offer, and that the money generated from the gambling industry will benefit the people by reducing dependency on welfare.

The Mohawk Warrior Movement's rationale for engaging in a gambling economy as a specific form of economy emerging from their sovereign right to economic self-determination has ignited a conflict revolving around individual sovereignty rights versus the Mohawk nation's collective sovereignty rights. Aboriginal sovereignty rights afford the Mohawk nation political and economic self-determination (the right to make decisions concerning issues that affect their society). Economic self-determination is itself considered a sovereignty right, and the warriors argue that engaging in the cigarette and gambling trade falls under the aboriginal sovereignty right of economic self-determination. Mohawk Warrior Movement opponents agree that economic self-determination is indeed an aboriginal sovereignty right. However, they argue that aboriginal rights are granted to and for the collective (collective sovereignty rights). Furthering one's own economic interests (individual sovereignty rights) is not an application or extension of sovereignty in their analytic framework. Further, the profits earned by the cigarette entrepreneurs and casino owners, many of whom are members of and/or use their earnings to support the Mohawk Warrior Movement, benefitted those individuals.

When questioned about the gambling opponents' assertions that the members of the Mohawk Warrior Movement are using the rhetoric of sovereignty to advance personal economic interests, Allan Delaronde replied, "It was never an issue of gambling or the money we could make from it. It's an issue of our land, and our people controlling it."

It is important to point out here that the Mohawk Warrior Movement's own actions at times tend to contribute to and perpetuate a conflicting ideology. The Akwesasne Mohawk Warrior Society supported and actively campaigned for Leo David Jacobs in 1988 and Lincoln White in 1989 as candidates for elected chief of the St. Regis Tribal Council. With the help of the Akwesasne Mohawk Warrior Society and other pro-warrior, pro-gambling constituents, both of these candidates won the positions they were running for. As pro-gambling Tribal Council chiefs, they have supported the business interests of the Mohawk Warrior Movement. It thus appears that some members of the Mohawk Warrior Movement may be as interested in individual sovereignty rights to support business interests as they are in the Mohawk nation's collective sovereignty rights. More importantly, refusal to recognize the state's jurisdiction over Mohawk affairs has been at the center of the Mohawk Warrior Movement's ideological argument in support of their legitimate sovereign right of economic self-determination (including the right to engage in a cigarette and gaming economy.) However, their newfound willingness to support a governing structure created and supported by the state in order to legitimate and protect their interests poses a fascinating question concerning the consistency of Mohawk Warrior Movement ideology.

It has been claimed that the bingo and gambling economy in Akwesasne had become so lucrative that by the end of 1987, "It was providing $7 million a year in tax-free profits to the owners of the six [gambling] establishments" (Johansen, 1993, p. 26). Further, by early 1989, ". . . gaming establishments at Akwesasne were generating more than $100 million annually in unreported income, operating totally without the sanction or supervisions of the tribal government" (ibid., p. 51). And that, by mid-1989, "Roughly 500 people were employed by gambling operations at Akwesasne, the largest source of employment on the reservation. One of every ten Akwesanse Mohawks . . . was working in a gambling establishment" (ibid., p. 34).

Bingo halls and casinos are legally permitted on reservations in the state of New York. However, slot machines are illegal. Nevertheless, the Mohawk Warrior Movement's refusal to recognize the state's jurisdiction has been at the center of the movement's ideological argument in support of sovereignty and their legitimate right to engage in economic self-determination within their national territories. Specifically, members of the Mohawk Warrior Movement believe that Canada and the United States are foreign nations with no authority to regulate the cigarette and gaming industries on Mohawk sovereign territory.

Opposition to the Mohawk Warrior Movement and its pro-gambling supporters grew during the 1980s. Violent confrontations between the pro-gambling and the anti-gambling factions began to occur. These confrontations escalated into the burning of bingo halls and casinos, as well as the shooting of firearms at owners and supporters of gambling establishments.

The Canadian federal and provincial governments were losing millions of dollars in unpaid taxes from the selling of discount cigarettes. Taking advantage of this factionalism, the Royal Canadian Mounted Police (RCMP) officers raided Kahnawake cigarette stores (*Montreal Gazette*, 1988a). On June 1, 1988, 200 RCMP officers invaded the Mohawk reserve of Kahnawake in an attempt to halt the sale of tax-free cigarettes. It has been suggested that "the cigarette trade was costing Canada $25 million a year in lost revenues" (Johansen, 1993, p. 29). Seventeen Mohawks were arrested, and $450,000 in cigarettes were seized (*Montreal Gazette*, 1988a). In response, members of the Kahnawake Mohawk Warrior Society seized the Mercier Bridge and closed every highway that passed through the reserve. They lifted the blockade after Canadian federal and provincial officials agreed to negotiate on the issue of discount cigarette trade. This event foreshadowed the blockade of the Mercier Bridge by Kahnawake Mohawks during the 1990 Mohawk-Oka conflict.

In 1989, the Akwesasne Mohawk Warrior Society faced a similar police crackdown on their lucrative bingo and casino business enterprises on the U.S. side of the reserve. New York state troopers raided seven casinos, hauling away slot machines and pressing charges against the owners for operating illegal gambling halls (*Malone Evening Telegram*, June 1, 1989).

This raid on the U.S. side of the Akwesasne Mohawk reservation differed in that economic self-determination is a right guaranteed in the Jay Treaty, which recognizes the Mohawks as a sovereign nation. This treaty has significant impact on other issues involving self-determination, such as the non-jurisdiction of the Bureau of Indian Affairs and local control of schooling. Yet, despite this treaty status, the machines were not returned and prosecution proceeded. Members of the Mohawk Warrior Movement saw in these two events further evidence of the need for direct action and the futility of reliance on legal recourse.

The events of 1988 and 1989 gave new support and legitimacy to the Mohawk Warrior Movement, as they were supported by hundreds of Mohawks who were infuriated by the massive police raid on their sovereign land. For those Mohawks who participated in the twenty-nine-hour armed standoff with provincial police officers, the confrontation was a powerful, personal experience that generated solidarity for future action. This was especially the case for one member of the Mohawk Warrior Movement, who wishes to remain anonymous:

> Many of us became warrior supporters . . . and for the first time picked up guns to help defend the community. . . . I could not have explained it if you asked me then. But looking back on it now, I can definitely say that my involvement with the movement was a direct result of that incident [the 1988 invasion and the resultant Mercier Bridge blockade]. I always knew in my head but for me that day, that day I really understood, understood in my heart that we could not allow any outsider to threaten our sovereignty and our right to determine for ourselves the direction we as a people, as a nation, should go. Whether it's a form of government or the way we choose to create financial independence. . . . But that day I saw how Mohawks standing together with a common purpose could fight for rights that are ours, ours by aboriginal claim. And I decided then that I would take a more direct approach, become more involved.

SUMMARY

The subsequent erecting of barricades and the supportive response and mobilization of Mohawks in the territories of Kanehsatake and Kahnawake during the 1990 conflict would emerge in response to the events and lessons gained during a twenty-two-year series of confrontations between the Mohawk Warrior Movement and the state (both Canadian and United States). In each case, the central confrontational issue linking the various mobilizations of support and conflicts were repeated attempts to preserve, defend, and extend the integrity of Mohawk nationhood. Experience had taught them the importance of political unity, the ability of sovereignty and nationhood issues to achieve that unity, and the benefits of direct action in attaining their goals.

By reviewing the historical, cultural, and organizational backdrop for the analysis of the 1990 Mohawk-Oka conflict, I have established the framework for and indicated the need to analyze the relationships among social networks, ethnic identity and consciousness, ideology, and social movement activity. Utilizing the voices of the participants, the next two chapters examine the Mohawk-Oka conflict that took place during the spring, summer, and fall of 1990.

6

Nations at War

Voice, Peaceful Resistance, and Mobilization

We have explored the importance of history, culture, and ideology as rallying points for mobilization. This chapter will review and analyze the precursors to and events of the conflict, which took place during 1990 between the Mohawk nation and the town of Oka, Quebec, Canada. This chapter will further demonstrate the importance of history and ideology for motivating and shaping movement participation and protest activity by incorporating the voices of participants, the members of the Mohawk nation who were involved in the conflict. These comments and insights will allow us to (re)frame the larger question of how social movement mobilization occurs and demonstrate how ideology (nationalism) and politicized ethnicity (ethnic identity and consciousness) can be transformed into a capacity for social movement activity. Thus, the chronology of events that follows is not meant to be an exhaustive account of the 1990 Mohawk-Oka conflict. Rather, it is a vehicle of exposition intended to carry forward the analysis in manners which both a) facilitates the exposition of motives, methods, and goals of participants, a process which illuminates the structural and instrumental influence of ideology and politicized ethnicity; and b) provides insight into how the framing of issues within the Mohawk Warrior Movement's framework of nationhood affected the sequence, context, breadth, and depth of social movement activities within this setting.

A BATTLE WITHIN A LARGER
WAR FOR NATIONHOOD

The 1990 Mohawk-Oka conflict emerged within a larger context of struggles between aboriginal peoples and the Canadian state. It is important to identify that larger context before undertaking the analysis of the particular events of the 1990 Mohawk-Oka conflict.

The conditions within Canada played a part in the escalation and intensity of both sides during the conflict. Recognizing this may further one's understanding of why the issues of autonomy and nationhood were so important to both sides involved in the conflict.

The failure of the Canadian federal and provincial governments to consider aboriginal nations as distinct societies and recognize their inherent right to self-government was directly indicated in the 1987 Constitutional Accord, the Meech Lake Accord. The Meech Lake Accord was an attempt at Canadian constitutional reform negotiated between the federal and the ten provincial governments. Initiated in 1987, it would have provided increased provincial powers for all the provinces as well as given the province of Quebec the political autonomy nationalists had been asking for by affording it "distinct society" status (Jenson, 1995). The Accord, which excluded aboriginal participation in the drafting of this constitutional reform, recognized the province of Quebec as "a distinct society" with separate linguistic and cultural rights. At the same time, the Accord denied "distinct society" status to First Nations' peoples within Canada.

One might argue that aboriginal opposition to the Meech Lake Accord contributed to its failure in June of 1990, engendering hostility toward aboriginal peoples from Quebec nationalists as well as from federal government officials. One can also argue that such hostility ultimately contributed to the provincial police and federal military invasion of Mohawk territory during the Mohawk-Oka conflict during that same year.

The Meech Lake Accord, which was drafted in 1987, had a June 23, 1990, ratification deadline (the date in which all provincial legislatures and the federal parliament had to ratify the Accord and elevate it to the status of a constitutional amendment). Seven of the ten provinces agreed to the Accord soon after it was drafted. Three provinces, Manitoba, New Brunswick, and Newfoundland, joined aboriginal leaders in their opposition to the Meech Lake Accord, arguing that aboriginal peoples deserved greater recognition in the Accord.

After much pressure, the provinces of New Brunswick and Newfoundland later supported the Accord. However, the province of Manitoba continued to resist, maintaining its coalition with aboriginal leaders who opposed the Accord because it failed to include them in the process of reform. Further, the Accord did not afford the same "distinct society" status to aboriginal peoples, nor did it include constitutional recognition for aboriginal land claims and self-government. In so doing, the constitutional reform continued to perpetuate the widely held myth that Canada consisted of two founding peoples, the French and the English.

The holdout provincial government of Manitoba agreed to hold public hearings regarding the content of the constitutional reform before it was put before the legislature for consideration. Native peoples and their leaders were among those who attended the hearings. Among them was Elijah Harper, a member of the Ojibwa-Cree community of Red Sucker Lake in northern Manitoba. Harper, a member of the New Democratic Party in the Manitoba Legislative Assembly, led an effort to prevent the Manitoba legislature from ratifying the Meech Lake Accord before the June 23 deadline by utilizing special procedural rules for considering constitutional amendments in the provincial legislature. In effect, he refused to give his consent to proceed with the constitutional reform measure through legislative action. As a result, the Meech Lake Accord failed to pass before the June 23,

1990, ratification deadline established at the constitutional reform conference held in the spring of 1987. Commenting on his
actions, Harper stated:

> We blocked the Accord because it posed a threat to aborigi-
> nal people. Aboriginal people have no quarrel with Quebec.
> But we're a distinct society too, and we've fought for many
> years for the basic rights that Quebec takes for granted, such
> as participating in constitutional talks (*Globe and Mail*, 1990)

His success in preventing the ratification of the Accord undoubtedly resulted in feelings of resentment directed toward aboriginal
peoples by the federal and Quebec provincial governments, contributing to the 1990 Mohawk-Oka conflict.

As one will see, the failure of the Meech Lake Accord resulted
in two positive outcomes for Canada's aboriginal peoples. First, it
enhanced ethnic consciousness and solidarity among aboriginal
peoples across Canada by uniting them in a common cause. Second, it created the basis for the widespread secondary protests and
blockades by other aboriginal peoples acting in support of the Mohawk Warrior Movement's efforts at resolving Mohawk land
claims and self-government issues during the 1990 Mohawk-Oka
conflict. Thus, the language frame of nationhood was especially
beneficial in mobilizing crucial resources because of the particular
historical context and previous mobilization.

THE 1990 MOHAWK-OKA CONFLICT

For more than two centuries, the Kanehsatake Mohawks have
been asserting their aboriginal rights to 154 square miles of land
that was expropriated for the use of the St. Sulpice religious settlement. Over the years, further land expropriation reduced the size
of what remained of Kanehsatake to 3.6 square miles. In 1989, the
size of the Kanehsatake Mohawk territory was in danger of being
reduced by forty-five acres or 2 percent of the remaining territory
in order to permit a golf course expansion project. With this

threat of further reduction of Kanehsatake Mohawk territory, members of the Mohawk nation engaged in various acts of resistance to protect the forty-five acres of traditional pine forest (referred to by Mohawks as "The Pines").

During a municipal council meeting in March 1989, Oka's mayor, Jean Ouellette, and representatives of the Oka Golf Club announced plans for the expansion of the privately owned, nine-hole golf course to be completed by the autumn of 1991. The town of Oka had purchased forty-five acres of "The Pines" for $70,000 from French owners of the land, Maxime-Maurice Rousseau and his brother Jean-Michel (Oka City Council, 1989). The Rousseaus were private land developers who held title to seventy-five acres of the 100-acre traditional Mohawk pine forest. The town had agreed to lease the land to the Oka Golf Club for the purpose of expanding the existing nine-hole golf course to eighteen holes. In addition, a $10 million housing development consisting of sixty luxury townhouses were to be built adjacent to the golf course (ibid.) The Rousseaus were to retain thirty acres of their original seventy-five acres for the purpose of building the townhouses.

During that same municipal council meeting, several townspeople asked Mayor Jean Ouellette, himself a member of the Oka Golf Club, if he had consulted the Mohawks before going ahead with the expansion plans for the golf course (*Montreal Gazette*, 1989a). Many residents of Oka opposed the golf course expansion and luxury housing development project because the golf course was a private club built on what they felt was public land. During that summer, 1,300 Oka residents, who were opposed to the expansion project for environmental reasons, signed a petition organized by environmentalists. They argued that any deforestation of "The Pines" would cause the sandy soil to erode.

For the Kanehsatake Mohawks, "The Pines" is a sacred place. But it is more than a place where they bury their dead. It is also a place from which they draw their spiritual strength and communal identity, where they practice the Mohawk way of life. Questioned about the importance of "The Pines," John Cree, spiritual faith keeper for the Longhouse, responded:

The Pines is a sacred place for me, for all Mohawks. It's like a church. The Pines is our sacred burial ground. We call it Onen'to:kon. It means "under the pines." We have been in this area for as long as we can remember. There's always been Mohawks here. It's part of our tradition. It is our sacred place. There's all kinds of medicines, and the trees are very old. It's our sacred land. It gives us pride, the Pines give us pride. This land . . . it is who we are. Without it we would not be Mohawks.

Immediately after Mayor Ouellette announced the plans for the golf course expansion project to the public, Kanehsatake Mohawks engaged in a number of peaceful demonstrations to show their opposition to the planned development. On April 1, 1989, more than 300 Kanehsatake Mohawks participated in an organized protest march through the town of Oka (*Montreal Gazette*, 1989b). These initial protests had little impact on stopping the golf course expansion project. As Walter David Jr., who took part in the occupation of "The Pines," explained:

> . . . we tried picketing and all that, but it seems the only way the world pays attention to us is when we pick up weapons, and we don't want to pick up weapons. If we try something peaceful, if we go in there quiet, they just push us off to the side. But if we go in there with weapons, they listen to us.

In another interview, Ellen Gabriel, spokesperson for the Mohawks behind the barricades at Kanehsatake, echoed a similar response:

> . . . we wanted to find a peaceful solution. That's why we held the protest march. We tried to get them to listen through peaceful measures. But they don't want peace. We could have had ten peaceful demonstrations, it wouldn't have mattered to them. The only thing they understand is the fist.

On August 1, 1989, the golf club's board of directors and expansion committee were to take part in a tree-cutting ceremony in "The Pines" to celebrate the expansion of the golf course

(*Montreal Gazette*, 1989c) With the media present and support from the Quebec Ministry of the Environment, more than 100 Kanehsatake Mohawks gathered in "The Pines" to protest the tree-cutting ceremony. Curtis Nelson, a Kanehsatake Mohawk who took part in the occupation of "The Pines," recalled:

> We warned them that if they cut down one tree, there would be consequences, real consequences. We also called for an end to all development on our land, not just the golf course expansion but any other projects on our territory until the land claim issue was resolved.

At the insistence of the Canadian federal Department of Indian Affairs and Northern Development (DIAND) and Quebec's Office of Native Affairs, Oka's Mayor Jean Ouellette agreed to a temporary moratorium on the golf course expansion development project in the disputed area (*Montreal Gazette*, 1989d). However, the warning given by the Kanehsatake Mohawks proved to motivate only a temporary delay in construction, rather than motivating Oka officials to seek a solution to the problem.

On March 5, 1990, the mayor of Oka and its municipal council lifted the seven-month moratorium and voted to proceed with the private golf club course expansion project (Oka City Council, 1990a). On March 9, members of the Oka Golf Club unanimously approved the decision to begin construction and hired a developer to construct the additional nine holes to the golf course, as well as the condominiums (*Montreal Gazette*, 1990a). More than 100 Kanehsatake Mohawks, supported by environmental groups that were demanding an environmental impact study, held yet another peaceful demonstration, this time outside of the golf club where the board of directors were meeting (ibid). Once again, the peaceful demonstration proved to be ineffective.

Fearing that there was not much time before construction of the golf course expansion was to begin, several Kanehsatake Mohawks orchestrated a strategy to stop the expansion project. In effect, the next day (March 10) the Mohawks of Kanehsatake began a twenty-four-hour surveillance and occupation of the area they call "The Pines." In an attempt to protest and prevent the town of Oka from expanding the golf course onto ancestral burial grounds, the Kanehsatake Mohawks erected a barricade along the Chemin du Mille, a seasonally used unpaved road leading to the forest (most of which was slated to be clear-cut for the expansion project) where the burial ground, the Pine Hill Cemetery, lies. This initial barricade was a small one made up of an old aluminum fishing shack, tree stumps and branches, and logs stacked across the dirt road. Marie David, a Mohawk from Kanehsatake who took part in the occupation of "The Pines," commented on the internal dynamics of the strategy employed:

> . . . strategy was important. But strategy is something that needs to be considered more. We need to learn more from struggles like this. We need to learn what works and what doesn't, what's the most effective.
>
> Unfortunately, when native people have to take a stand, it's generally at a time when there's not really a lot of time to develop a [long-term or in-depth] strategy. Like this particular incident . . . it was more spontaneous than planned out. We had to just immediately set up a roadblock without thinking if it was the best strategy.
>
> We knew we had to keep them out, we had to protect "The Pines." It was more instinct than strategy. . . . As far as strategy . . . I think incidents like this are going to make us a little more strategic in the future because these incidents haven't ended completely at all, they'll still continue. And we have to be ready, we have to think more about strategy.

The town of Oka's lawyer, Luc Carbonneau, argued that the Mohawks were illegally blocking the dirt road going through "The Pines" (*Montreal Gazette*, 1990b) Specifically, the town of Oka argued that this road, known as Chemin du Mil, was a municipal thoroughfare. In agreement, on April 26, the Quebec Superior Court in St. Jerome ruled that the Mohawks were illegally preventing the development of the land and granted Oka's initial request for an injunction barring Kanesatake Mohawks from continuing their barricade protest of the golf course expansion project (Quebec Superior Court, 1990a).

The Mohawks, however, chose to ignore the court ruling and continued the barricade protest. As Kanehsatake Mohawk Ellen Gabriel explained:

> We don't recognize the authority of the province over our land. We weren't about to let an injunction prevent us from defending our land. It didn't matter to me how many injunctions they had. We had no intention of obeying the court order. We were protesting to protect our land, our sacred land. Our people had to stand up to the encroachment, we just had to.

During the next three days, the Surete du Quebec (SQ, Quebec's Provincial Police) were deployed along Highway 344, a main road that crosses Kanehsatake Mohawk land.

During the early part of June 1990, members of the Mohawk Warrior Movement from the Mohawk territories of Akwesasne, Ganienkeh, and Kahnawake began to arrive in Kanehsatake. With them they brought communications equipment, weapons, and other material resources that would later prove to be essential to the struggle. They also brought other types of (non-material) resources such as a sense of responsibility to history, a collective ethnic identity and consciousness, and an ideology that would prove to be equally essential components to the struggle. While the Kanehsatake Mohawks favored the extent of support the Mohawk Warrior Movement afforded them in their struggle, not all Kanehsatake residents favored the presence and use of weapons.

The Oka Municipal Council hired private demolition contractors to enforce the court injunction and remove the Mohawk barricades. Perhaps it was because they feared a confrontation with Mohawks in front of television cameras that the Oka Municipal Council postponed the dismantling of the Mohawk barricade that was to take place on May 1 (*Montreal Gazette*, 1990c). Instead, after the Mohawks requested to meet with the minister of Indian affairs, Tom Siddon, both sides agreed to discuss possible solutions concerning the removal of the Mohawk barricade.

On June 21 and 22, there were a series of meetings held between individuals who assumed the responsibility of representing
federal, provincial, municipal, and Mohawk nation interests.
Agreeing to meet at a designated spot in "The Pines," municipal
representatives included Oka municipal councilman Gilles Landreville and Oka municipal lawyer Luc Carbonneau. Mohawk nation representatives included spokespersons Ellen Gabriel and
Johnny Cree (*Montreal Gazette,* 1990d). Federal representatives
included Pierre Coulombe, who represented both Quebec's Prime
Minister Robert Bourassa and his Indian affairs minister John
Ciaccia, and Yves Desilets, a federal official from the Canadian
Ministry of Indian and Northern Affairs (ibid.).

According to interviews with a number of Mohawks, throughout the two-day negotiating session, Oka municipal councilman
Gilles Landreville insisted that the land belonged to the municipality of Oka and that the municipality had the right to lease the
land to the Oka Golf Club. However, the Mohawk protesters
would not back down from their claim to the land. As a result, the
negotiations produced a stalemate. The stalemate was inevitable
because each side refused to concede the issue of land ownership.
As Kanehsatake Mohawk Curtis Nelson explained:

> Our position was we were open to discussions but they
> would have to be conducted in the proper context, on a
> government-to-government basis, and long-term solutions
> would have to be found. It became evident fairly quickly
> these talks would not go far . . . they [the federal govern-
> ment representatives] would not take our position seriously
> . . . and refused to recognize our traditional Longhouse gov-
> ernment. . . . The government sees they need land, and
> their first thought is to take it from the Indian people. We
> explained to them to expand the golf course on Mohawk
> land was a total disregard for Mohawk people, for all native
> people. We were willing to take down our barricade, but
> only if the government guaranteed The Pines would not be
> destroyed. They had to guarantee the golf course would ex-

pand someplace else. . . . We explained to them we negotiate on political differences, not aboriginal rights They wouldn't accept the idea the land was not a negotiable issue.

Denise David-Tolley, a Kanehsatake Mohawk who took part in the occupation of "The Pines," commented:

> . . . what they wanted to do was take a sacred burial ground of the people of Kanehsatake, burial grounds we have used for thousands of years, burial grounds we still use today, and they wanted to use it to expand a golf course. We were not willing to back down, to give up our burial grounds. They just couldn't understand its importance to us. All they could see, all they wanted to see, was a golf course bringing in more people and more money. . . . They are always wanting to use our land when they have other lands available to them. They always take our land first. This time we weren't going to let them do that. And they just couldn't understand.

During the second day of the negotiation process, Mohawks spotted the Surete du Quebec flying several helicopters over the Mohawk barricade. The Mohawk protesters became suspicious that these activities were preparations for an attack to gain control of the disputed land. Fearful of a provincial police invasion, the Mohawks broke off further negotiations and asked the Akwesasne and Kahnawake Mohawk Warrior Societies for help in maintaining the barricade, in protest of the golf course expansion.

The network relationship that exists among the Mohawk territories enabled the Kanehsatake Mohawk protesters to call on the Mohawk warrior societies from Akwesasne and Kahnawake for additional technical support and expertise. The members of the Akwesasne and Kahnawake Mohawk Warrior Societies had been more politically active in their own reservation territories. As a result, they had greater experience, leadership, and resources (weapons and communication technology) which they brought to the Kanehsatake protest.

The conflict also created additional opportunity for recruitment into the Mohawk Warrior Movement. Motivated by a sense of history, some participants recalled how land had been stolen from an older generation of Mohawks, and they felt a sense of responsibility to not let this happen again. While commenting on what motivated him to participate, Ronald Cross, a member of the Kanehsatake Warrior Society, explains the significance of history and past struggles:

> . . . I didn't want it to be like it was with my ancestors . . . being forced off traditional lands. We didn't want that to happen again. We always said we would never let it happen again. We have always known we were cheated out of our traditional territory, but this time we weren't willing to let that happen again.
>
> Putting up those barricades, we developed a stronger sense of pride. Protecting what was left of our territory, we regained a sense of history. Acting on knowledge of our history, we regained some of our strength, our power. Putting up those barricades, protecting our land—that gave us power. Acting on our history—that gave us power. History can be a very powerful thing. It's our history that was important to what we did. It's our history that gives us power, acting on our history is power.
>
> I became a warrior because it gave me a chance to make history mean something, to make up for a history that cheated us out of our territory. I saw it [movement membership] as a real opportunity to do something, as a way to stand up for Mohawk rights, to show the government they couldn't take our land without a fight. . . . There was a coming together, and I wanted to be part of that. There was a unifying effort in the community . . . on the barricades . . . to fight the golf course. We had strong support from the community.
>
> It was the warriors who gave us that support, who gave us strength to fight. They gave me the chance to fight for the land, to fight for all Mohawk people, to defend the rights of the Mohawk nation. . . . I became a warrior because it gave

me a chance to make up for history, it gave me a chance to fight to make history different this time.

In another interview, Kanehsatake Warrior Society member Dennis Nicholas reflected on his membership and offered the following:

> . . . when I stopped to think about what came before, I couldn't imagine myself not participating, not standing up for my rights, for Mohawk rights. When I think of our history, of the history forced on us. . . . I guess it's probably because of the things that had been done to my mother that I've been made aware of in the past. Her being taken away from her family and being forced to go to Indian brainwashing school. Being told over and over again her people were savages and she couldn't use her native language and she'd be beaten when she did. It's that, all these things—what has come before—that brought much more desire to do whatever I can, in whatever way I can, to help right some of the wrongs that have been committed against Mohawks, against all native peoples. It's because of our history, a history of wrongs against our people, that I, that all of us, became warriors.

These interview passages reflect the participants' recognition that history and a sense of responsibility to that history became a causal factor in the 1990 Mohawk-Oka conflict. This sense of historical responsibility developed from a knowledge base of past injustices and struggles. This knowledge has been transmitted from generation to generation through membership in one's clan. It has also been taught to younger generations of Mohawks through the Mohawk controlled school at Kahnawake, which Mohawk children from both Kanehsatake and Kahnawake attend. Dale Dion, a member of the Mohawk Nation Office in Kahnawake, which is the political voice of the Longhouse there as well as that of the Kahnawake Warrior Society, explains:

> Our clans have many responsibilities. They are not only responsible for teaching us who we are as Mohawks . . . but also

what has come before. This starts when one is very young, almost immediately. . . . We are taught Mohawk history . . . how our nation has had to fight for survival . . . what we had and what has been taken from us. We are taught about the land, about our ceremonies, about our responsibilities as Mohawks to the nation.

We continue to teach this in our school. Before we had our school, this was not the case. . . . Now Mohawks are taught Mohawk history . . . not some white version of Mohawk history. They are taught the realities of what has happened and that they must not let it happen again . . . that they have a responsibility to the future of the Mohawk nation. . . . We cannot rewrite our history, but they are taught, as we all are, that we can make good on it, on past injustices, by living up to our responsibilities as Mohawks to never let it [past historical injustices] happen again.

The Mohawk Warrior Movement capitalized on this sense of historical responsibility to encourage membership and protest participation.

A second and related factor that motivated participation within the Mohawk Warrior Movement was the way the conflict and participation was framed. Throughout the confrontation, the members of the Mohawk Warrior Movement justified their actions in terms of ideology (the ideology of Mohawk nationalism), claiming to defend Mohawk nation sovereignty by protecting Kanehsatake and Kahnawake from invasion by foreign (Quebec and Canadian) governments. Once potential participants understood that the issue was the defense of Mohawk territory and framed it in terms of nationhood, they rallied to the cause with a singular sense of purpose, becoming members of the movement. Commenting on what motivated him to participate, Kahnawake Warrior Society member Randy Horne voiced the following:

I never gave much thought to the warriors, never considered myself to be a member before the golf course problem. When I saw them with no fear, standing up to Canada, I wanted to be part of that too. . . . They gave me a sense of knowing who I am, a stronger sense of cultural identity and meaning. They gave me a political purpose, the fight for Mohawk nationhood. They made me understand it was about more than the golf course. They made me understand that it was about nationhood, Mohawk nationhood.

That political purpose was seen in "The Pines" in everyone's faces. For me, it started there, and it still continues today. As long as our territory continues to be taken away from us, I will have political purpose. As long as it's a matter of Mohawk nationhood, I will have political purpose, I will fight for that political purpose.

In another interview, Dean Horne, who is also a member of the Kahnawake Warrior Society, echoed a similar sentiment::

My involvement . . . the barricades in "The Pines" . . . was for Mohawk nationhood, the right of all Mohawks to exist as a separate and independent nation. When I thought about it in terms of Mohawk nationhood . . . it was then I understood I had a responsibility to become a warrior, a responsibility to fight for Mohawk nationhood.

In the above interview passages one can see that nationalist ideology became a second causal factor in the 1990 Mohawk-Oka conflict. Participants' actions were, in part, based on the ideology of the Mohawk Warrior Movement. Specifically, participants internalized this ideology, which movement leaders had framed both the movement's and the conflict's mobilization around.

Further, this seems to support Klandermans' (1994) notion of transient collective identities. From the above interview passages one can see that as more nationalist-minded leaders and members of the Mohawk Warrior Movement joined the resistance activities, the collective identity of the protest participants reformulated from a group of Mohawks defending a burial ground into an identity marked by a deeper cultural resonant theme—a Mohawk nationalist collective identity. Participants' sense of cultural, or collective identity, and protest activities then became refocused on sovereignty and defending sovereign boundaries from what was then perceived as outside foreign forces.

Led by Guy Dube, non-Mohawk residents of Oka who sup-ported the golf course expansion project organized in opposition to the Mohawks and formed a group called Rassemblement des Citoyens d'Oka (roughly translated as Oka Citizens Assembly). On May 8, during a municipal council meeting, Ressemblement des Citoyens d'Oka demanded that the municipality of Oka take title to the disputed land and begin construction of the golf course expansion project (Oka Municipal Council, 1990b). In response to pressure from the citizens' group, Oka filed its second request for an injunction barring Kanehsatake Mohawks from continuing their barricade protest of the golf course expansion. However, on June 7, the Quebec Superior Court in St. Jerome denied the re-quest for a second injunction (Quebec Superior Court, 1990b). Instead, the Court ruled that negotiations should be given an-other try.

According to Mohawk respondents, a week later federal Indian Affairs official Yves Desilets and provincial Indian Affairs repre-sentative Pierre Coulombe attempted a second try at negotiation with Mohawk protesters, but again there was no movement in ei-ther side's position. By this time, Oka officials were growing impa-tient. Both they and Rassemblement des Citoyens d'Oka took an increasingly hard line as the Mohawk protesters refused to back down, continuing their barricade protest.

On June 30, after more than three months after filing its initial court petition and winning a temporary injunction, the Quebec Superior Court in St. Jerome responded to the municipality of Oka's third request to end the Mohawk protest. In so doing, the Court issued yet another temporary injunction ordering the Mohawks to dismantle their barricade at Kanehsatake (Quebec Superior Court, 1990c). On July 2, the Oka Municipal Council, through its lawyer Luc Carbonneau, then applied for and received provincial permission to remove the Mohawk barricade by use of force if the Mohawks did not comply with the provincial court-ordered injunction (*Montreal Gazette*, 1990e). Then, on July 10, Oka Mayor Jean Ouellette requested that the Surete du Quebec (SQ, Quebec's Provincial Police Force) remove the Mohawks' barricade. Linda David-Cree, a Kanehsatake Mohawk who took part in the occupation of "The Pines," recalls the Mohawks reactions:

> When word of the government's position got back to the people in The Pines, many were angered. They felt we had tried peaceful and diplomatic ways to have Canada take us seriously. They decided it was time to fight and the barricade would not come down until Canada relented. Some of us disagreed with this approach because we felt other peaceful avenues could be explored. . . . We tried repeatedly to arrive at a consensus on how to achieve our objective, but to no avail. . . .

Canadian and United States (as foreign nations) laws are not recognized as legitimate within the traditional national territories of the Mohawk nation. As such, the Kanehsatake Mohawks ignored the provincial court's injunction to dismantle the barricade. Instead, the Mohawk protesters prepared for a violent, armed confrontation with provincial police. With the help of the Mohawk Warrior Movement, the Kanehsatake Mohawks constructed a stronger barricade, fortifying it with logs and barbed wire. They also established a radio system of communication that linked members of the Mohawk Warrior Movement in Kanehsatake with their counterparts in Akwesasne and Kahnawake and organized a twenty-four-hour armed patrol to defend their territory in Kanehsatake.

SUMMARY

This review of the process of peaceful resistance and mobilization shows the importance of history and nationalism as motives for resistance. Second, for members of the Mohawk nation, the historical processes of protest and negotiation and the intransigence of the Canadian federal and Quebec provincial governments both

reflected and, in effect, amplified the nationalist frame. The setting and context "struck a chord" of familiarity due to the content
of their education and their culture of resistance. In other words,
they recognized that similar contests had occurred before and that
they were part of an ongoing continuum. Because these events
struck a cord of familiarity, history became transformed into personal motive. In effect, the Mohawks realized that they (and their
ancestors) had engaged in this struggle before—making them part
of the historical struggle and obligating them to respond. It created a familiarity that motivated otherwise disinterested individuals into participation and even membership in (or identification
with) the Mohawk Warrior Movement. Had members of the Mohawk Warrior Movement from the other Mohawk territories
entered into a community that lacked this culture and these interpretations of previous events, they might have been viewed as
troublemakers rather than allies defending the land and national
rights.

Further, Mohawk Warrior Movement leaders successfully mobilized protest participants by drawing on deeply resonant cultural
themes and traditions early on in the conflict. By framing the protest activity in a way that resonated with the culture of the
Mohawk nation (with members' sense of identity and ideological
orientations), movement leaders appropriated long-standing cultural beliefs and values regarding one's sense of responsibility to
Mohawk history and right to sovereignty. This cultural legitimacy
attached to protest activities during the 1990 Mohawk-Oka conflict encouraged movement participation and facilitated and
maintained subsequent mobilization later on in the conflict.

Finally, the nationalist framework allowed Mohawks to mobilize and/or acquire material resources needed for a struggle that
otherwise would have been beyond their limited economic and
political resources. These resources included weapons, strategic
experience, and media connections. Each of these resources are
identified in the social movement literature as important factors
influencing the mobilization, maintenance, and success of a social

movement, and access to all were made possible because Mohawks recognized their collective commonalty and drew upon their shared interpretation of this event in the larger continuum of nationalist resistance.

7

Nations at War

Voice, Armed Resistance, and Maintenance of Mobilization

The peaceful occupation continued until the early morning of July 11, 1990, when over 100 Surete du Quebec police officers (SQ, Quebec's provincial police force), under orders from Oka Mayor, Jean Ouellette conducted a paramilitary assault on the 300 Mohawk men, women, and children protesters in order to enforce the court injunction to dismantle the Mohawk barricades (*Montreal Gazette*, 1990f). From the open encampment near the cemetery, Mohawk protesters could see what they estimated to be 100 to 120 Surete du Quebec officers with flak jackets, gas masks, bulletproof vests, and rifles, standing by their vehicles parked on Highway 344.

The Quebec provincial police fired tear-gas canisters and concussion grenades into the encampment, then opened fire with automatic rifles. The Mohawk protesters shot back in self-defense. It is important to note here that not all of the 300 Mohawk protesters were members of the Mohawk Warrior Movement. Debbie Etienne, one of the Kanehsatake Mohawk protesters behind the barricades that morning, recalls the attack:

They [the SQ] started to attack us during our morning [to-bacco-burning] ceremony. I could see the smoke blowing toward the barricades, and they started coming over and I saw them, and I said they're coming in, they're coming in. And then it was at that point that they opened fire. We really didn't expect it, not like that. You know from the beginning we expected a confrontation, but we didn't expect the intensity of the attack. We expected to be met with the riot squad and dogs or something and be dragged away in which we were perfectly willing to get arrested like that. . . . They insisted later on that they were only shooting over our heads, but the bullet holes in the trees are at chest-level, so there's no way they weren't shooting to kill us.

Another Kanehsatake Mohawk protester, Denise David-Tolley, also describes the attack:

They [the SQ] first started firing the tear gas. It exploded all around us. We couldn't breathe, our eyes were burning, our throats were burning. It was complete confusion. Then they fired the bullets. Our men hadn't even fired one shot back yet, but when the bullets kept coming, they opened fire too.

Although the attack by the Surete du Quebec police on the Mohawk barricades described by these Mohawk respondents seemed endless, it lasted only twenty-four seconds (*Montreal Gazette*, 1990g). In the exchange of gunfire, a provincial police officer, Corporal Marcel Lemay was shot and fatally injured. Police and Mohawk versions of the shooting varied sharply. The Mohawks contend that the police officer either shot himself accidentally or was shot by other officers. The Surete du Quebec claim that Corporal Lemay was gunned down by a Mohawk who leaped out of a trench in the woods, firing at a group of officers (ibid.) However, even after a year of forensic testing, it remains uncertain as to who fired the shot that fatally injured Corporal Lemay, as both the SQ and some of the Mohawk protesters were using the same type and caliber of semiautomatic rifle that day.

With the death of the police officer, the provincial police re-treated and regrouped at the bottom of the hill on Highway 344, leaving behind several police vehicles, including two vans, four patrol cars, and an earth-moving machine intended to dismantle the Mohawk barricades. One can only surmise that they were sur-prised by the extent of Mohawk firepower. Brenda Gabriel, an-other Kanehsatake Mohawk who took part in the occupation of "The Pines," commented on the police action:

> All I can say about it is that we were certainly surprised by their choice to retreat. I guess they were caught off guard by our strength. I don't think we realized ourselves how strong we were . . . that we could actually fight them off. But we did . . . and then we started to believe in our strength. I know we didn't have the numbers that they did . . . but we were deter-mined to hold onto our land . . . protect The Pines . . . stand up for our aboriginal right. When we saw them run back we understood that we had control of The Pines. From that point I knew it would be different.

The Mohawk protesters used the abandoned earth-moving ma-chine to overturn the police vehicles, fortifying their position by erecting a barricade on the crest of the hill on Highway 344 over-looking the town of Oka. They also created roadblocks at the northern entrance on Centre Road and farther west on Highway 344 near the junction of St. Germain Road, thus protecting all entrances to the disputed land and the rest of Kanehsatake. Mohawks then took control of the nine-hole golf course that abutted the disputed land, raising the red-and-yellow Mohawk Warrior Movement flag over the club's manicured lawns.

In an act of solidarity with the Kanehsatake Mohawks, Mohawks from the Kahnawake reserve, near Chateauguay (a south shore suburb of Montreal) eighteen miles southeast on the southern shore of the St. Lawrence, set up barricades on three ma-jor highways, leading to and from Montreal, which cross their re-serve. Those roads included Highway 138 (two miles southwest from the center of Kahnawake), Highway 132 (a mile and a half east from the center of Kahnawake), Highway 207 (three miles south from the center of Kahnawake), and the paved road known as Old Chateauguay Road. In addition, the Kahnawake Mohawks seized the Mercier Bridge, which rises from their land near the town of Chateaugay, Quebec. That bridge is a major commuting route connecting Montreal and several suburbs on the south shore of the St. Lawrence River. They threatened to blow up the bridge if the police launched another attack on Mohawks in Kanehsatake.

This show of solidarity opened a "second front" for the Surete du Quebec. It also demonstrated the vulnerability of modern society to violent challenge. Specifically, it transformed a twenty-minute commute into a three-to-four-hour commute for the 60,000 commuters who use the Mercier Bridge every day to drive to and from downtown Montreal from the south shore suburbs. Additionally, Kahnawake Mohawks occupied the Kanawaki golf course, an exclusive club located on leased land belonging to the Kahnawake Mohawks.

Richard Two Axe, a member of the Kahnawake Warrior Society, commented on this act of solidarity:

> The police had to fight us on two fronts. They could not isolate us as a group of militants in the woods. They had to see us as a major political problem, a political force. . . . We had yet to decide on any long-term strategy. It was more of a spontaneous thing, a tactic that had worked for us in the past. We only knew that we had to do something, and we were counting on this. When you look at it, what else could we have done, it wasn't a choice to do it or not. To the outside we are Mohawks from Kahnawake, Mohawks from Kanehsatake, but we are more than that, we're all part of one Mohawk nation.

This commitment to supporting the struggles of the Kanehsatake Mohawks is expressed in the following statement made by Kanehsatake Warrior Society member Ronald Cross:

> None of our Mohawk people stand alone in struggles for jurisdiction and sovereignty over our lands. We are all part of

one Mohawk nation, and an attack on one part is an attack on all of us. We've lost too much territory. Not just us [at Kanehsatake], all of us. It wasn't just for us, it was for all of us, for all native nations everywhere. It's the same issues, the same fight. We have to stand together, support each other, fight together. Let them know they cannot break us apart, We are different nations, but we are also one.

Jean Catafard, another Kanehsatake Warrior Society member, explained the tactics of solidarity used:

We weren't about to be bullied into losing more of our aboriginal territory. We were determined to show Canadians that we would stand up for our rights, aboriginal rights, and that we were not afraid. We wanted to show them that we were committed to armed resistance to protect those rights. They shouldn't underestimate our determination to protect our rights.

We weren't just Kanehsatake Mohawks fighting for a pine forest and graveyard. We were fighting for more than that . . . fighting for Mohawk nationhood. We were Mohawks as a nation standing up for all of our rights. . . . And we felt that the bridge was the place to start. We felt that we could convince the SQ [provincial police] that we would blow up the bridge if they attacked a second time. And they wanted that bridge back in one piece, they needed it. So as long as we controlled the bridge, we had a lot of power. It was their fear of what we would do to that bridge that gave us part of our power.

The Mohawk-Oka conflict, especially the police attack on Kanehsatake, engendered an enormous display of aboriginal unity. Indigenous peoples from all across Canada and the United States who had and continue to experience similar land rights and nationhood issues, rallied to support the Mohawk Warrior Movement and the Mohawk nation. This solidarity with the Mohawk nation was of two types. Some people showed their support in the form of sympathy protests and blockades of roads and railways across Canada. These earliest acts of solidarity were spontaneous responses by individual aboriginal nations; however, subsequent acts of support were more formally organized. Ojibways from the Long Lake reserve in northern Ontario blocked a section of the Trans-Canadian Highway and the Canadian railway that runs through their reserve, effectively stopping transcontinental rail traffic for over a week. This blocked one of the major avenues for moving freight in Canada. Algonquins from western Quebec occupied an island on the Ottawa River. The St'latl'imix from the Seton Lake reserve in British Columbia erected barricades across seven roads and railway lines that pass through their reserve, including the railway line between Vancouver and Prince George that links the urban areas of the southwest coast. Aboriginal peoples in Alberta threatened to destroy hydroelectric transmission lines. Micmacs in Nova Scotia held protest marches and hunger strikes. And aboriginal peoples in Manitoba demonstrated in front of the Manitoba Legislature in support of the Mohawks.

Other indigenous individuals traveled to Kanehsatake and Kahnawake and joined the Mohawks behind the barricades. In an interview with an Ottawa-Chippewa supporter of the Mohawk cause from the urban Indian community of Detroit, Mickey "Two Eagles" Bulmer explained why he joined the Mohawks at the barricades:

> It's important that all Indian people stand together as one . . . united to defend our rights. When we stand together, it makes us all stronger, we can accomplish more. That's why we all went there to support them. Oka has continuously happened throughout history . . . it is happening right now in the Canadian northwest with logging . . . right here in the states with mining. It's something that we have all faced some time or another, in some way or another.

In another interview, Nancy Wonshon, a Chippewa from Detroit, offered her reason for joining the Mohawks behind the barricades:

> Oka was a reminder to what has happened to all of us and an opportunity to act against it. It symbolized something we all believe in—the struggle to defend our land and our rights.

Not only did the Mohawk-Oka conflict became a universal symbol of the encroachment of the white man onto aboriginal land, but the Mohawk resistance also was symbolic of their own struggles to defend aboriginal rights.

Later in the day, on July 11, in order to prevent any reprisals, reinforcements totalling more than 1,500 provincial police officers were sent to seal off the entire area surrounding Kanehsatake, more than one-third of the entire 4,000-member Quebec provincial force (*Montreal Gazette*, 1990h). These provincial police officers then constructed checkpoints throughout the area, establishing ten of their own barricades. Two of these were set up directly opposite the Mohawk barricades on Highway 344, the main route through Oka, at the eastern and western entrances to Kanehsatake to prevent Mohawks from entering the town of Oka (ibid.) They set up additional barricades on Centre Road along the northern edge of the disputed land, as well as on other strategic roads, trying to prevent the arrival of reinforcements from other Mohawk reserves (ibid.) They also had two boats that patrolled the Ottawa River which borders Oka's south and west edges of town. It was at this point that Kanehsatake became a "police state." Further, 500 SQ officers and 300 Royal Canadian Mounted Police (RCMP, Canada's national police force) sealed off the Kahnawake Mohawk territory, setting up a barricade on Highway 138 in Chateauguay, just outside the Kahnawake reserve, as well as one on the northern side, or Montreal side, of the Mercier Bridge (ibid.) The SQ barricade on Highway 138 was patrolled with the support of the local Chateauguay police force.

As the SQ surrounded both Mohawk territories, non-native residents of adjacent Chateauguay (a town of 40,000 residents), angry at the Kahnawake Mohawks for blocking the Mercier Bridge, gathered nightly throughout the months of July and August to show their opposition to the Mohawk's barricades. Shouting racist remarks and burning effigies of Mohawks, the 1,000 to 2,000 participants in these protests frequently became violent. Although the police stood by watching the Chateauguay protesters, on one occasion however, the Quebec riot police were called in to quell a massive riot, as nearly 2,000 residents tried to dismantle the police barricades.

On July 12, informal talks began between the Quebec provincial government and several clanmothers and other Mohawk nation representatives, including members of the Mohawk Warrior Movement (*Montreal Gazette*, 1990l). Quebec Prime Minister Robert Bourassa sent Quebec's minister of native affairs, John Ciaccia, to negotiate a solution to the conflict. Meeting with members of the Mohawk Warrior Movement behind the Mohawk barricades, both Ciaccia and the Mohawk warriors discussed a proposal put forth by the Mohawk nation. According to Kahnawake Mohawk negotiating group member Joe Deom the Mohawks' demands included the following:

> . . . complete withdrawal of the SQ [from Kanehsatake and Kahnawake]. Participation by the federal government in discussions regarding the land dispute with the Mohawk nation on a nation-to-nation basis. There had to be a guarantee that no arrests would be made [for the shooting and seizure of the Mercier Bridge]. We also wanted a permanent agreement that the golf course wouldn't expand [into The Pines]. There also had to be a fair solution to the land claim issue once we did remove the barricades

According to various respondents, Ciaccia would not agree to the Mohawks' third demand (that no arrests would be made) but did promise that if the Mohawks removed their barricades the police would not attack. The Mohawks reaffirmed their defensive position that the SQ police force had to completely withdraw from both Mohawk territories before the barricades would come down.

Three days later, on July 15, a tentative agreement was reached that was acceptable to both sides. Both sides agreed to a two-phase withdrawal of the Surete du Quebec police force—half of the more than 1,000 officers were to withdraw from Mohawk land, resulting in the removal of the Mohawk barricades, followed by the complete withdrawal of the remaining SQ police force (*Montreal Gazette*, 1990j). In addition, Ciaccia agreed to support a federal initiative that would grant the Mohawks rights to their burial ground in "The Pines," as well as resolve the land claim issue dating back to the eighteenth century (ibid.).

For the past two decades, the militancy of Canada's indigenous population has resulted from frustration over stalled efforts to resolve land claim issues. Before 1973, the Canadian federal government did not recognize indigenous land rights. Only after a five-year court battle by the Nishgas of British Columbia did Canada change its indigenous land claim policy and begin to consider the rights of indigenous peoples to their traditional land. In 1973, Canada instituted two types of land claims, comprehensive and specific. Comprehensive land claims can be filed by indigenous nations that have never signed treaties to surrender their land rights. Specific land claims can be filed by indigenous nations on the grounds that the federal or provincial government has violated a treaty pertaining to land rights. Despite this change in Canadian-aboriginal land claims policy, the process for addressing indigenous land claims has been slow.

The next day, July 16, the agreement was declared void by the Mohawks (*Montreal Gazette*, 1990k). The Mohawks, outraged by news reports that the SQ provincial police force would be replaced with Canadian armed forces, felt the government had violated the agreement. As a result, the situation was at a stalemate—the Mohawks refusing to dismantle their barricades and the government authorities threatening a second attack.

In an attempt to diffuse the crisis, Federal Indian Affairs Minister Thomas Siddon announced on July 26 that the federal government was negotiating a deal to purchase the 100 acres of land intended for the golf course expansion project and the luxury housing development, in order to then give it to the Kanehsatake Mohawks (*Montreal Gazette*, 1990l). Funding for the purchase was to come from the ministry's budget for settling native land claims. The federal government was willing to pay the town of Oka $3.8 million for seventy acres of "The Pines" it owned, plus one dollar for the Mohawk cemetery (ibid.) In addition, the federal government was also willing to pay $1.4 million to land developers

Maxime-Maurice Rousseau and his brother Jean-Michel for the thirty acres (sixty residential lots) of "The Pines" that they owned on which they were to build luxury houses (ibid.) The federal government would then turn over the land it had purchased to the Kanehsatake Band Council. However, on July 31, Oka Mayor Jean Ouellette and the Oka Municipal Council refused the government's offer to buy the disputed land (Oka Municipal Council, 1990c). Further, it was a deal that the Mohawks did not embrace. Their argument was that the land was theirs and that there would be no justice in using what was in effect Indian money to buy Indian land. As Kanehsatake Mohawk protester Linda Gabriel explained:

> They didn't get it, they didn't understand that our land was not for sale. There are no papers anywhere where [sic] Quebec or Ottawa can prove that we ever sold our territory. Never, there's no documents anywhere. So how could Oka sell land and Ottawa buy land that wasn't theirs to begin with? We never sold this country, we never will.

On August 5, Quebec's Premier, Robert Bourassa, warned the Mohawks that they had forty-eight hours to disarm and dismantle their barricades before he would order a military attack (*Montreal Gazette*, 1990m). Preparing for what they felt would be an inevitable second attack, the Mohawks decided to let the ultimatum deadline pass.

The Quebec provincial government issued a response to the Mohawk's continued defiance. Claiming that the Mohawk's continued resistance was a threat to Quebec's security, Quebec Premier Robert Bourassa requested federal intervention. On August 8, after a joint statement with Premier Bourassa, Canadian Prime Minister Brian Mulroney invoked Canada's National Defense Act (*Montreal Gazette*, 1990n). He announced that more than 4,000 federal troops (Canadian armed forces) were on standby to replace the Surete du Quebec provincial and Royal Canadian Mounted Police at both Kanehsatake and Kahnawake (ibid). The decision to deploy federal troops was the first internal deployment of Cana-

dian armed forces since 1970, when the Canadian federal government, under the administration of Prime Minister Pierre Trudeau,
invoked the Canadian War Measures Act and called out the
troops to mobilize against Quebec militant separatists, the Front
de Liberation du Quebec (FLQ).

Within hours of Prime Minister Mulroney's announcement,
Oka Mayor Jean Ouellette and the Oka Municipal Council met to
reconsider the government's offer to purchase the disputed land.
In a surprise move, the council agreed to sell the disputed land to
the federal government, thereby aborting the golf course expansion project that would have destroyed much of "The Pines," including the Mohawk burial grounds (Oka Municipal Council,
1990d).

However, for the Mohawk nation, the issue was now much
larger than the golf course expansion project. This larger issue,
voiced by a number of Mohawk respondents, was a demand for
recognition of Mohawk nationhood. Here, the nationhood frame
actually reframes or redefines the 1990 Mohawk-Oka conflict,
from a particular to a symbolic event. The Mohawks had "won"
the particular battle, but by buying into their own mobilization
rhetoric they risked and, in part, "lost" the symbolic struggle. The
nationhood frame for recruiting movement members reframed the
movement and the conflict. As Robert Skidders, a member of the
Akwesasne Warrior Society, expressed:

> When we first put up the barricades the issue was "The Pines."
> It started with the golf course expansion and in a lot of people's
> minds it ends with the golf course expansion. But it went be-
> yond the issue of the golf course. In the end it was a fight that
> had very little to do with a golf course. It was a fight for nation-
> hood, Mohawk nationhood. It became a war against the Mo-
> hawk nation, against Mohawk sovereignty, against all native
> people. We want the right to make our decisions about our
> land. That's what it was about. We began to put it in the con-
> text of our nation demanding sovereignty, of a political situa-
> tion and a matter of rights that needed to be addressed as the
> Mohawk nation to the Canadian nation.

Allen Gabriel, a Kanehsatake Mohawk who took part in the occupation of "The Pines," echoed a similar sentiment:

> . . . the golf course was an important issue, don't get me wrong. But you have to realize that the real struggle was about our identity, Mohawk identity. It was about the sovereignty of the Mohawk nation, about our responsibility to Mohawk sovereignty. . . . That's where our future lies, where our power lies, in our identity and sovereignty.

This sentiment was also supported by Kanehsatake Warrior Society member Joe David who stated:

> We have always asserted our sovereignty, even before our first encounters with Europeans. We have never stopped thinking of ourselves as a sovereign nation. Our actions were an assertion of our legal jurisdiction over our land, of our sovereignty. . . . It is Quebec and the rest of Canada who refuse to recognize our sovereign status. We have always maintained our sovereignty. Our barricades were more than preventing a golf course. They were an assertion of our nationhood and the right to determine what happens to our land. The attack on our barricades was an attack on our nationhood; there can be no mistake about it. That's how we see it, that's how it is.

Still yet another Kanehsatake Mohawk protester, Kelley Tolley, voiced the following:

> . . . to defend the land is to defend nationhood. Land and nationhood cannot be separated . . . they are the same. Without land, without territorial jurisdiction, there is no nation. They saw it [the land] as a golf course. We see it as more than that . . . as aboriginal right . . . the right to exist as a nation.

Once again, one can see the importance of Mohawk Warrior Movement ideology (nationalism) as a causal factor in the 1990 Mohawk-Oka conflict, as well as the change in participants' sense of collective identity. Participants acted, in part, based on an ideology of nationalism.

While the Mohawk Warrior Movement was supported by many Mohawks, it did not speak for all Mohawks. There were Mohawks who opposed both the Mohawk Warrior Movement's economic and political agenda as well as tactics during the conflict (Alfred, 1995). In fact, pockets of opposition within the Mohawk territories of Akwesasne, Kahnawake, and Kanehsatake intensified regarding the Mohawk Warrior Movement's role in the Mohawk-Oka conflict. Opponents of the movement contend that their role in the conflict was masking the movement's real intentions, arguing that movement leaders intentionally manipulated support for Kanehsatake and Mohawk land rights issues in order to advance their own economic and political agenda. This opposition partly stems from the continuing internal conflict (factionalization) between the Mohawk traditional Longhouse and Canadian-imposed, Elected Band Council governmental systems that exist simultaneously within the Mohawk territories.

Kanehsatake's elected Grand Chief George Martin and his fellow Band Council members led the opposition to the Mohawk Warrior Movement. Martin made his opposition known to the public when the media reported that he gave Loran Thompson, a member of the Akwesasne Warrior Society and part of the movement's leadership structure, the following warning:

> Get your warriors out of my reserve. This is not your reserve. I'm the Grand Chief. This is my reserve. . . . Let us do our business. . . . (*Montreal Gazette*, August 3, 1990)

Additional opposition to the Mohawk Warrior Movement was expressed when the Kanehsatake Mohawk Negotiating Team (a coalition of Akwesasne, Kahnawake, and Kanehsatake Mohawks) requested the Assembly of First Nations of Canada to put an end to the movement's participation in the Mohawk-Oka conflict and negotiations. The coalition's request to the organization, which represents almost 600,000 aboriginal peoples across Canada, stated:

> Since July 14, the Mohawk people of Kanehsatake have attempted to cooperate with the negotiation process organized

by the Mohawk nation warriors' negotiators, but have become increasingly concerned that they were not being given a significant role; were not permitted to involve their own advisors; and that the issues of direct concern to the community in the areas of land and jurisdiction were not being addressed. . . . We have made repeated attempts to cooperate with the warriors' negotiators to ensure that the voice of the majority of the Mohawk people is clearly heard and understood, only to be rebuffed, insulted, and abused. This refusal by the warriors' negotiators to accept the clearly defined priorities of the Mohawk people of Kanehsatake does not respect the inherent authority, rights, or aspirations of our people. . . . (Kanehsatake Negotiating Team, Communique to the First Nations of Canada, August 21, 1990)

Four days later, on August 23, a group of Kahnawake Mohawk women also voiced their opposition to the Mohawk Warrior Movement's role in the Mohawk-Oka conflict. Their opposition, which was circulated in a community letter to Mohawk residents within Kahnawake, stated:

Many people in Kahnawake, Kanehsatake, and Akwesasne believe that the present blockade crisis is out of hand and is indeed in the wrong hands. . . . They [Elected Band Council] should not assume that the majority of the community has accepted the warriors/nation office as leaders/spokespeople for the Confederacy. What is indicated is people's disgust as the Mohawk council of Kahnawake continues to abdicate responsibility and authority to a self-interested, small but aggressive faction in the Mohawk communities. It is time to question whether we have been manipulated into a situation of supporting the warriors/nation office who, we should remember, are the same people who defied community will, ignoring consensus on numerous occasions. . . . They used the Kanehsatake land issues as a catalyst to get community support. . . . (Women of Kahnawake, To All Kanienkehaka in All Mohawk Territories, August 23, 1990)

Their statement makes reference to the lack of acceptance on some Mohawks' part concerning the Mohawk Warrior Movement's image as spokespeople for the Iroquois Confederacy. What their statement is referring to here is that throughout the conflict (and prior to the conflict as well) there was a great deal of confusion concerning who the spokespeople were, not only for the Iroquois Confederacy but for the Mohawk territories of Akwesasne, Kahnawake, and Kanehsatake. This confusion results from the movement's own self-image and language, which includes the use of such words as "Mohawk Nation" and "Iroquois Confederacy" when speaking about the movement in terms of socioeconomic and political issues concerning Mohawks. In fact, the Iroquois Confederacy's Council at Onondaga and its Canadian counterpart at Grand River have not conferred upon the Mohawk Warrior Movement any responsibilities that would lead one to believe that they were indeed spokespeople for all members of the Iroquois Confederacy. This also raises legitimacy questions concerning the Mohawk Warrior Movement in the sense that, despite its status as an official organization of the Kahnawake Longhouse, it is not a universally accepted organization of the larger Mohawk territory as a whole. As such, for whom they speak and the exact extent of their importance to the Mohawk nation are, at the very least, issues in a muddled debate.

Now that the issue was much larger than the golf course expansion project, formal negotiations between the Mohawk Nation and both the Quebec provincial and Canadian federal governments began on August 16, in an effort to reach a peaceful solution to the Mohawks' demand regarding the recognition of Mohawk nationhood (*Montreal Gazette*, 1990o). According to respondents, four days later, however, the Mohawks once again called off the talks, arguing a breach of trust. This breach of trust was specifically in response to the use of force by the Canadian government, in this case, the deployment of Canadian armed forces.

On August 20, after forty days of duty at the barricades in Kanehsatake and Kahnawake, the 1,500 Surete du Quebec provincial police officers withdrew from their positions (*Montreal Gazette*, 1990p). They were replaced by 1,500 soldiers from the Canadian armed forces. The troops, in armored personnel carriers, positioned themselves along Highway 344 in Oka/Kanehsatake and Highway 138 in Chateauguay/Kahnawake, within ten yards of the Mohawk barricades (ibid.). Prior to military intervention, the distance between the SQ and Mohawk barricades was approximately 1.5 kilometers, or one mile. Consolidating their new positions closer to the Mohawk barricades, the military began to set up razor wire fences approximately five meters directly parallel to the Mohawk barricades which surrounded both territories. An additional 2,500 soldiers remained at four strategic locations within ten miles of Oka and Kanehsatake, as well as Chateauguay and Kahnawake (ibid.).

On August 21, formal negotiations between the Mohawk nation and the Quebec provincial and Canadian federal governments resumed (*Montreal Gazette*, 1990q). However, these negotiations would resume and collapse on and off for several days. Feeling that they could no longer negotiate a peaceful solution, three days later, on August 24, Quebec Premier Bourassa called the talks off permanently because both the provincial and federal governments would not agree to engage in discourse with the Mohawk nation concerning the broader political/economic issues on a nation-to-nation basis. Mavis Etienne, a member of the Kanehsatake Negotiating Team, commented on these demands:

> We knew things had to change and felt that it was the best time to do that. We felt that if we pushed hard enough we could get more than the golf course. So we put all our grievances on the negotiating table. We wanted more than just the return of The Pines. We also wanted them to engage in a nation-to-nation relationship between us and them. We knew we were asking Canada to rework its entire approach to native affairs, but we felt we had to do this. This was about our rights. Recognize our rights, all of our rights, not just some.

Arguing that the negotiations to peacefully remove the Mohawk barricades had reached an impasse, on August 27 Quebec Premier Bourassa formally requested that federal armed troops remove the Mohawk barricades at Kanehsatake and Kahnawake (*Montreal Gazette*, 1990r). That same day, military officials prepared to execute a military invasion of both Mohawk territories. In doing so, the Canadian armed forces sealed off all entrances to both territories, marking the start of military operations to remove the Mohawk barricades.

Two days later, on August 29, an unexpected agreement was reached between the military and a group of Kahnawake Mohawks who controlled the Mercier Bridge, resulting in the dismantling of the Mohawk barricades that blocked the entrance to the bridge. Several Kahnawake Mohawk Warrior Movement members agreed to help dismantle the Mohawk barricade on Highway 132 near St. Catherine (*Montreal Gazette*, 1990s). A short time later, the Mohawk barricade on Highway 138, serving as a physical border between the town of Chateauguay and Kahnawake, was also dismantled in a joint effort (ibid.). Once the Mercier Bridge was open, it was under complete military control as the military occupied the bridge and highways that led to and from Kahnawake. However, the Mohawks still had barricades in place guarding the entrances that led into the heart of Kahnawake. An interview with a Kahnawake Warrior Society member, who wishes to remain anonymous, explains the decision to help the soldiers dismantle the barricades:

> We really believed that there was a chance to win, a chance for things to change, and we wanted to take it. But it was going to have to be another day, in another way. We knew that this was just a small part of the fight . . . the larger issues would still have to be fought for. So while we gained some control, weakened the hold of Canadian authority over us some amount, we still had a ways to go. . . . I guess maybe the real win in all of it was that we came together as a nation even stronger than before. And I would have to add that it will serve us well in the future, in future battles with Canada.

Our chance for real change will come about because of our stronger identity and unity.

On August 31, Kahnawake Longhouse women walked to the barricades guarding the community as an act of solidarity with the Mohawk Warrior Movement. They expressed their support for them in the following joint statement:

> Our people of Kanehsatake and Kahnawake have been acting in good faith. Our people have given and are still giving the governments of Canada and Quebec every opportunity to avoid a violent confrontation and find a peaceful resolution to the situation we have been in resulting from the armed attack by the Surete du Quebec Police on Mohawk men, women, and children in Kanehsatake.
>
> We have come together today to show our support for the men, Rotiskenrahkete, The Carriers of Peace, who, through their dedication to the Mohawk nation, have put their lives on the line. It [coming together in support] is also for the same reason—to protect and defend our territories, our land, the women and children, our nation. As women, we stand behind our men who are carrying out their duties and responsibilities.
>
> We also wish to show our support for those negotiators who have acted in good faith in meeting all the terms of the governments in order to sit down at the table. The world must see that we stand together as the Mohawk nation, and we will not fall under the iron fist of the oppressive police state and military aggression which Premier Bourassa and Prime Minister Mulroney have initiated.
>
> We, the Mohawk women, have our duties and responsibilities as mothers and keepers of the land and stand alongside our men (Rotiskenrahkete) in this time of defending the Nation. (Mohawk Women of Kahnawake, Joint Statement to Community, August 31, 1990)

However, as discussed earlier, the Mohawk Warrior Movement did not engender this level of support from all Mohawk women, nor even all Mohawks.

The next day, on September 1, the Canadian Army entered the heart of Kahnawake and invaded the Longhouse, searching for weapons that members of the Mohawk Warrior Movement might have hidden there. The army also established checkpoints at all entrances to the reserve (*Montreal Gazette*, 1990t). The standoff at Kahnawake was over.

The Mohawk barricades at Kanehsatake, however, remained in place as the Mohawk Warrior Movement was committed to defending "The Pines." However, two days later, on September 3, Canadian armed forces invaded Mohawk territory once again (*Montreal Gazette*, 1990u). Surete du Quebec police officers came in behind the army and took control of Kanehsatake, placing it under military and police occupation (ibid.). Without a shot being fired, the fifty Mohawk protesters left behind the barricades (thirty of whom were members of the Mohawk Warrior Movement) gave up the main barricade at the top of the hill on Highway 344 that they had built to defend their territory. Two other Mohawk barricades, one protecting the northern entrance of Kanehsatake and the other guarding the western entrance, though still intact, were abandoned a few days prior to the army's invasion. The army dismantled all the Mohawk barricades, gaining complete control of Kanehsatake. The government, with its greater resources in terms of manpower and weapons, was in a better position to prevail.

In the confusion that ensued, the thirty Mohawk Warrior Movement members, as well as the twenty women and children, managed to evade the soldiers and barricade themselves inside the community's Drug and Alcohol Rehabilitation Center (Onen'to:kon, or "Under the Pines"). It was a last act of resistance. All negotiations between the Mohawks inside the treatment center and the Quebec provincial and Canadian federal governments continued to reach a stalemate. But on September 26, after more than six months, the Mohawk resistance ended when the thirty Mohawk Warrior Movement members, accompanied by the twenty women and children carrying flags of the Iroquois Confederacy and the movement, walked out of the treatment center (*Montreal Gazette*,

1990v). Their decision to leave was not an act of surrender but rather an act of completion, in that they had accomplished their task of awakening the world community to the larger political issues concerning the Mohawk nation, as well as all indigenous nations.

When it was over, the soldiers had arrested fifty men, women, and children. Dragging them onto buses, they were transported to the military police base in Farnham, Quebec, where they were held in custody and interrogated without the presence of a lawyer. Forty of those people arrested were arraigned on charges of obstruction of justice, firearms violations, and/or participating in a riot (*Syracuse Post Standard*, 1990). Eventually, after the passage of much time, they were released, the women and children first, then the men.

Although the conflict between the Mohawk nation and the state had a devastating impact on the Mohawk territories, there were also many positive outcomes. Throughout the conflict a renewed spirit of community solidarity developed among the Mohawks, as well as a resistance to outside aggression. Commenting on her experience, Kanehsatake Mohawk protester Linda David-Cree voiced the following mixed emotions:

> It brought the community together . . . and that will make us strong. I suppose it will make all of us stronger. Maybe in that way something good did come from it. Yes, I think it did; it really did after all. I guess it's how you define it that matters. . . . And I'd say we're stronger. Coming together made us stronger, stronger for now and stronger for next time.

In another interview, Kahnawake Mohawk elder Rita McComber commented on the positive gains:

> . . . I'd have to say that what happened here, our struggle—it unified the Mohawk people. It brought a pride. It helped to instill a pride in many of our people in who they are and where they are. It wasn't that pride wasn't there to begin with, but it increased an awareness of who we are. It forced us to come together and unite and just in that respect it helped bring out more pride. . . . It encouraged our people to become involved in the political aspects of our people and the gov-

ernment-to-government relationship and the recognition of sovereignty. It helped to bring all native people together.

Valerie David, a Kanehsatake Mohawk who took part in the occupation of "The Pines," said:

I'm not sure that we won something, just not sure that we accomplished anything. Are we better off than before it all happened? I would have to say not really. Are we in control of our land, our economy, our right to self-government? No. ... Yes, the golf course won't destroy our Pines [or] our burial grounds, but nothing is changed. Everything is the way it was before. Only when we have the right to decide for ourselves how we should be governed, the right to decide what economy is best for us, the right to exist as a sovereign nation, then we will have accomplished something, then we will be in control of ourselves. Only then will we have power.

Dale Dion, a member of the Mohawk Nation Office in Kahnawake, commented on the experience:

Many of our children are going to grow up having seen what happened here, remembering what happened here. They will be able to tell the next generation what it meant to stand up the way we did, to see ourselves as sovereign and independent despite the defeat and betrayal. That's one power we still have, and we showed the whole world that we're willing to exercise our right to our land and our right to protect ourselves from those who choose not to see us as a nation. ... A nation never dies unless the people are willing to let it die. And we were not willing to let the Mohawk nation die. We did what we needed to do to keep it alive, to keep it strong, to keep it sovereign.

SUMMARY

The unifying sense of commonalty and community expressed by the Mohawk respondents derives from having a conscious knowledge of being deprived of aboriginal rights. This shared experience, combined with a knowledge of history and a sense of responsibility to that history, provides the basis for identity and consciousness formation. In turn, this experience generates conditions favorable to Mohawk activism.

The usefulness of movement leaders, in general, to protest movements depends on their ability to mobilize constituents. Language has been identified by social movement theorists (Benford, 1993; Hunt and Benford, 1993) as an important factor for mobilizing and guiding participants in social movements. Here we have seen that Mohawk Warrior Movement leaders were effective conduits for the articulation of group grievances Specifically, they used a language of liberation—the ideology of Mohawk nationalism—to articulate group grievances against state repression. Here, the language frame was both a method of amplification and a focus identifying the primacy of one particular value, in this case, nationalism or nationhood. Articulating a language frame with an implicit political agenda and strategy that stressed the maintenance of territorial boundaries and regaining pre-existing (aboriginal) civil, social, political, and economic rights, assigned meaning to Mohawk Warrior Movement activity. And within that particular cultural and historical setting, the ideology frame elicited widespread support for protest activities. Further, the language frame not only amplifies and therein help to retain and expand support for the movement, but can also have feedback that causes the movement to reframe itself and its goals.

This book's focus on language frame extends frame amplification in three ways. First, it delineates a specific case in which rhetoric, or language, focuses on a value. Second, it identifies how that language acts as an amplifier, giving participants a louder voice by virtue of their language selection. Third, by amplifying "so loud" that it causes a change in, or modification of, the behavior and goals of the movement, language reverberates as frame "feedback" and reformation. Further, language framing was also instrumental for escalating and maintaining the mobilization process during the 1990 Mohawk-Oka conflict because even individuals within the Mohawk nation who had been critical of the Mohawk Warrior Movement in the past became members when participation was equated with a Mohawk's responsibility toward the Mohawk nation. Thus, a language (ideology) frame is a useful resource for social movements in that it can generate and/or expand a committed constituency.

The Mohawks interviewed in this study have located the 1990 Mohawk-Oka conflict within the context of a pre-existing historical conflict and ongoing struggle. Mohawk history established material and legal basis for claims of Aboriginal rights and nationhood. Participants reacted not merely out of a sense of injustice but out of a recognition of economic and legal possibility. This conflict serves as a conceptual or interpretive framework in which participants acted upon deeply-held beliefs, while assigning symbolic (as well as particular) meaning to protest activity. As the Mohawk Warrior Movement mobilized against the Canadian state as a socially and politically self-conscious movement, the nationhood-based ideology became an important resource. By synthesizing constituency goals with an effective ideology, Mohawk Warrior Movement leaders successfully mobilized ideological commitments held by members and non-members of the movement alike. Via the ideological frame of "nationhood," Mohawk Warrior Movement leaders were able to assign meaning to movement participation and protest activity, and reframe the 1990 Mohawk-Oka conflict over a golf course into a rationale and strategy of resistance. While on the surface the 1990 Mohawk-Oka conflict was over land, the struggle for nationhood underlies the motives, methods, course, and goals of that conflict. Therefore, for Mohawks, the interpretive framework that reshaped protest action was that of "nationhood." Further, the ideology of nationalism was reinforced through symbolism. Specifically, symbolic actions such as the building of barricades and the bridge blockade, used as border controls establishing group boundaries, were directed at reaffirming Mohawk nationhood, and thus became part of the interpretive framework.

Ideology and consciousness are distinct, but related, concepts. Ideology is a product of cultural traditions (Tucker, 1989). Consciousness is a product of history and experience. It involves an awareness or reinterpretation of one's experiences and/or conditions. Together, ideology and consciousness constitute a framework for linking thought to action. Interview data demonstrate the significance of ethnic identity and consciousness for Mohawk Warrior Movement activity. Specifically, members of the Mohawk territories sustain a collective identity and consciousness that motivates them to act in defense of their aboriginal rights. This identity and consciousness is constructed and maintained through a common history of oppression and domination. Further, not only were ethnic identity and consciousness found to be key factors in motivating participation, but they shaped the strategies of resistance.

Although a knowledge of and sense of responsibility to one's history, politicized ethnicity, and ideology were found to be essential pre-conditions and important resources for mobilizing a constituency, it was also found that this was not a sufficient condition in and of itself for maintaining mobilization. Resource mobilization theorists have argued that the passage from "condition" to "action" is, in part, contingent upon the availability and amount of resources under a group's collective control and its ability to mobilize such resources (Gamson, 1975; McCarthy and Zald, 1973; 1977; Oberschall, 1973; Tilly, 1978). A material and organizational resource base was also required. Specifically, resources such as group organization, social networks, a committed membership, the ability to finance activities, weapons, and outside support were equally important. In other words, while nonmaterial cultural resources may have been the seed bed, other types of resources were needed to fertilize that seed bed. It is not enough to be able to act on one's history, identity and consciousness, or an ideology. Rather, in order to act on those cultural abstracts, a movement must have tangible resources as well.

Cultural resources such as history, identity and consciousness, and the language (ideology) frame of nationalism solicited additional sources of support for mobilization—other indigenous peoples, the media, individuals and groups who brought food and other provisions to the barricades, and so on. Thus, for groups who are oppressed and resource deficient in the context of the dominant society and the resource mobilization paradigm, these non-material conditions become an essential method for acquiring the additional resources necessary to carry their movement through a struggle.

8

Politicized Ethnicity and Nationalism

Conclusions

Reflecting on the 1990 Mohawk-Oka conflict, the influence of politicized ethnicity and ethno-nationalist ideology within the Mohawk Warrior Movement and its potential for facilitating movement activity is clear. This synthesized and modified theory has shown an ability to explain the processes of member recruitment, mobilization, and maintenance, and the motives, methods, (changing) goals, and successes of this social movement. It has demonstrated greater explanatory power than any of the three dominant social movement theories—resource mobilization, new social movements, and frame analysis, as isolated explanations.

Gurr's (1993) explanatory model of ethno-political action provided key insights that were helpful for analyzing the Mohawk Warrior Movement. In his study of ethno-political conflict and mobilization against the state, he indicates that a group's historical loss of political and economic autonomy, awareness of discrimination, and cultural or ethnic identity contribute to the formation of group grievances (p. 123). However, he fails to identify the motives or methods by which some grievances become important contests and/or escalate to violence at some times and in some settings, and not in others.

This book suggests that one needs to go beyond the axiomatic assumption that "recognition of cultural loss and lost opportunity" motivates social movement action. Specifically, this book shows that it is one's knowledge of and sense of historical responsibility and obligation to losses of land and sovereignty (in conjunction with a politicized ethnicity) that encourage people to participate in and mobilize around the issue of a proposed golf course expansion/land seizure in Mohawk nation territory. As the interviews indicate, history became a causal factor because members of the Mohawk nation located this contest within a continuum of conflict, and that interpretation evoked a sense of obligation and responsibility. History as motive was predicated on a particular knowledge about both the history of this land and of this struggle, the role of land in that cultural and cosmological context, and the interpretation of the legalistic efforts by actors imbued with an oppositional culture.

The interviews and my analysis also show that the Mohawk Warrior Movement leadership was a crucial factor in encouraging participation and mobilization of social movement efforts. Their emphasis on locating contemporary events within that continuum and promoting a particular interpretation was crucial to cultivating a commitment to and support of many Kanehsatake residents and Mohawks on other reserves for direct confrontation at Oka. Thus, it is not just the cultural loss, but the perception within a context meaningful for the particular ethnic group that matters.

Resource mobilization theorists (Gamson, 1975, McCarthy and Zald, 1977) identified both the importance of acquiring and utilizing resources and the amount of resources under a group's collective control as crucial (and indeed seemingly determinant) factors in a social movement's ability to mobilize and succeed. These theorists have shown the importance of focusing on the mechanics and conditions of a social movement—how it works—but have paid insufficient attention to explaining why people participate. Herein, one learns that the reasons why people participate can constitute a basis for creating, borrowing, or substituting for needed mechanics.

The Mohawks, although traditionally resource-deficient, were extremely effective in gaining access to needed resources. The manner by which the Mohawk Warrior Movement gained those resources was particular to their own group history, the larger historical context (including Meech Lake), and the existence of particular networks that were endemic to and hidden from most analysts. Further, they used a particular ideology to elicit the offering of resources by individuals, groups, and agencies, many of which were uninvolved (in any direct manner) in the conflict.

The nationalist ideology within this historical context was used by the leaders of the Mohawk Warrior Movement to secure material support, including weapons and strategic knowledge. It also helped movement leaders to secure access to media coverage and, in turn, to secure support from other actors who became allies and engaged in secondary contests. This analysis shows that while denial of access to resources may be the kiss of death to movements as resource mobilization theorists claim, one need not have, nor control, those resources as long as one gains access to them through a loan by others, and/or if one gains the benefits of their operation in manners supportive of one's efforts.

Similarly, resource mobilization theorists have emphasized the importance of formal social movement structures as a factor in movement success. Several other social movement scholars have argued and demonstrated the importance of less formal social networks for facilitating protest activity (Fantasia, 1988; Klandermans & Oegema, 1987; McAdam, 1988; Morris, 1984). Social networks are thought to facilitate the likelihood of movement participation because they facilitate group cohesion through interaction with similar others, knowledge of movement activity, and contact with recruiting agents (McAdam, McCarthy, & Zald, 1988).

This book indicates the importance of examining the content and influences of culturally specific informal networks among the participants and underlying the operation of the movement. In this book, it was demonstrated that the organization, mobilization, and maintenance of Mohawk Warrior Movement activity was predicated on the network-like communal clan system of the larger Mohawk nation. This network integrated people from within each, as well as among, the Mohawk territories based on their family and friendship ties, and it created an effective communication system. This type of social network facilitated a multi-layered sense of commitment and responsibility to living friends and relatives, as well as to ancestors or historical actors, by movement participants. As Tilly and Shorter (1976) have demonstrated, layered and interdependent systems are particularly resilient when challenged and resistant to interruption or fracture.

This particular type of integrated social network structure overcomes the criticisms about and limits of segmented, polycentric integrated networks (SPINS) (Gerlach 1983). Instead of the polycentric decentralized structure impeding or restricting the coordination of the larger Mohawk Warrior Movement, it actually facilitated coordination among peoples with a similar upbringing and expectations, by encouraging a sense of community, commonality, and solidarity for its members—factors essential to collective identity (Touraine, 1985; Melucci, 1989, 1994).

This study suggests that informal social networks do much more than encourage participation and embed identity. The Mohawk Warrior Movement leaders used these networks to secure and mobilize material resources. Examples of how informal kin and clan networks facilitated Mohawk Warrior Movement activity include providing financial support (with money from the cigarette and gaming economy), acquiring weapons, securing strategic knowledge, promoting secondary confrontations, and gaining media access.

Despite the fact that indicators of the traditional methods and forms of resource mobilization commonly found in unions and class-based social movement (as specified by the resource mobilization theorists) were absent, this does not mean that the existence and mobilization of resources was trivial or tangential. It is important to recognize that the mechanisms, motives, and methods by which resources were identified, selected, and marshalled occurred in cultural-specific and cultural-appropriate manners.

For this case in particular, for most oppressed ethnic minorities, and perhaps for resource-deficient groups in general, resource mobilization is a secondary factor in the emergence, course, and conduct of the armed social struggle. And the form and function of such efforts may occur in manners distinct from those specified by analysts focusing on institutions of the dominant society and those involving long-established, hierarchical, and formally constituted social movements.

Snow, et al., (1986) and Snow and Benford (1988) have argued the need to look beyond material resources and have emphasized the importance of actor interpretation or perceptive frame. Snow and Benford (1988) have emphasized that social movements frame or assign meaning to and interpret relevant events and conditions in ways that are intended to identify, analyze, and convey issues, as well as to mobilize constituents (p. 197–98). Further, as Klandermans (1989;9) has noted, social movements are "producers of meaning," in that they become conduits for the articulation of (constituency) values and beliefs, goals, and grievances. The Mohawk Warrior Movement leaders (acting intuitively) recognized this need and were able to produce and convey meaning by articulating an ethno-political ideology that emphasized history and nationhood. By offering an explanation that resonated their constituency's values and beliefs, goals, and grievances with movement interests and goals, movement leaders were able to rally their constituency to act in support of the protest activity at Oka. This approach operated in manners similar to Snow, et al. (1986) theory of frames; ". . . individual and social movement interpretive interests, values and beliefs and social movement activities, goals, and ideology become congruent and complementary" (p. 464).

Another non-resource approach championed by Cohen (1985), Downey (1986), Eyerman and Jamison (1991), Whittier and Taylor (1991), Melucci (1988, 1994), and Mueller (1987) has stressed the importance of collective identity to movement development. Further, Cornell (1988a) and Nagel and Snipp (1991) have argued that for indigenous peoples, collectivity arises from efforts that involve the politicization of First Nation peoples particular to the issues of aboriginal rights. My analysis of the Mohawk Warrior Movement and the 1990 Mohawk-Oka conflict supports those insights.

A sense of collectivity was crucial to the formation of a politicized ethnicity (ethnic identity and consciousness) and transformation of members of the Mohawk nation into political actors. The formation of collective identity emerged among participants in various Longhouse organizations, especially the Kahnawake Longhouse Singing Society and different warrior organizations. Specifically, that sense of collectivity was based on an understanding of the systematic causes of oppression and the importance of recognizing one's place in a larger historical continuum. It made resistance to oppression an intrinsic element of collectivity and therein formed the basis of an oppositional culture. This context of ethnic and historical consciousness encouraged the transformation of members of the Mohawk nation into political actors pursuing the common interests of the Mohawk nation as they collectively understood it. Thus, collectivity, arising from this highly politicized context, encouraged Mohawk Warrior Movement mobilization due to a sense of responsibility.

Further, for the protest participants, this "transient" collective identity (Klandermans, 1994) changed over the duration of the conflict as additional movement leaders and members entered the resistance activities. Participants were no longer political actors merely pursuing a common interest of protecting a burial ground. They became political actors, focused on resistance activities tied to a collective identity of Mohawk nationalism. This transient collective identity was facilitated by the language frame used by movement leaders as a vehicle of movement strategy and maintenance. However, this approach pays insufficient attention to the role of resources and issues of movement maintenance, coordination, and strategy.

As is hopefully apparent by now, none of the three dominant social movement theories alone can explain the complex developments during the 1990 Mohawk-Oka conflict. Resource mobilization, new social movements, and frame analysis theories, when combined, can contribute to an analysis of social movement activity that has more explanatory power (explaining both the "how" and "why" of social movement activity simultaneously). However, it is important to note that even when combined, these approaches are still wanting. Specifically, neither approach takes into consideration the primacy of history (a group's knowledge of and sense of responsibility to its history)—or the source of social movement activity found to be essential in this case study of Indigenous, ethno-political struggle against the state. Further, both the resource mobilization and frame analysis approaches pay insufficient attention to the issue of collectivity and the rationale and methods of initial politicization and formation of an oppositional culture.

My analysis of both the Mohawk Warrior Movement and the 1990 Mohawk-Oka conflict demonstrates that politicized ethnicity and ideology are important interpretive frameworks that serve as rallying points facilitating social movement activity. Critical to this analysis is an understanding of how history, and a group's sense of responsibility to that history, becomes a catalyst for social protest. Furthermore, this analysis found that not only are these cultural resources contributing factors to social movement activity, but they also, in conjunction with material and organizational resources (such as group organization, a kinship network structure, a committed membership, the ability to finance activities, weapons, and outside support), are essential for facilitating and maintaining social movement protest.

While it is probable that all of these factors will not be significant in all social movement activities, ethno-political conflicts, or indigenous struggles, the identification and their interactive effects and impacts in one of the more dynamic and high-profile events of this decade, suggests the need to treat these attributes as factors to be considered (but not assumed) when explaining such social movements. While the particulars of the cases and dynamics will surely vary from situation to situation, and case to case, the demonstrated interaction of these multiple factors underlying and facilitating social movement activity, supports the contentions of Ferree and Miller (1985) and Klandermans (1984) regarding the need for an integrated social movement framework and constitutes one contribution toward such an integrated approach.

When asserting the importance of a theory, one must ask whether the case is so unique that it offers a particular insight that may operate in all but are rarely observable. Or, is it sufficiently common that findings from it are easily generalizable. This case study itself has what might seem unique properties: First Nations' peoples losing land for a golf course development project. However, a brief review of events has suggested that even at the most particular level, this is not a unique attribute. Modavi (1992) noted that a golf course expansion project was also a contributing factor in and a catalyst to social movement activities by native Hawaiians. Bradley (1995) suggested that the rise of the Green political party in New Mexico and the forging of an alliance of indigenous peoples and progressives was also precipitated by the seizure of indigenous land for a golf course development project. During the summer of 1995, Japanese farmers protested a similar development and emphasized the trampling of long-standing land occupancy and rights (National Public Radio, 1995).

Less specifically, the contests over land claims in particular and sovereignty in general are at the heart of most ethnic conflicts. There is nothing in the structure of social movements or ethnic groups that would immediately suggest that the basic insights into the role of history, identity, oppositional cultures, and informal and ethnically particular social movements might not be potential factors affecting event development. Thus, while it would be irrational to assume the applicability of this synthesized theory or any of its elements to other struggles, it is, however, appropriate to treat the theory and its components as part of a potential explanation and, as such, factors to be considered (but not assumed) when conducting such analyses.

SUMMARY

The events of the 1990 Mohawk-Oka conflict are not over. Relations between the Mohawk nation and the Canadian federal and

Quebec provincial governments continue to be difficult, with the causes of the conflict remaining unresolved. Canada has done little to address or resolve the fundamental issues that contributed to this conflict. It is still a potential site for additional confrontations. Land rights issues remain unresolved and continue to fester. By consistently choosing to avoid the examination of treaty issues in earnest, the government of Canada has failed to recognize that it is the part of the Crown that bears the responsibility contained in the historic treaties. As a result, the recent unresolved conflict between the Mohawk nation and the state indicates that First Nations will not be immune from ethno-nationalist conflicts in the future, but rather continued systematic political and socio-economic indiscretions against aboriginal peoples will continue to generate indigenous, ethno-nationalist reactions.

The significance of this book, then, lies in highlighting the important role that politicized ethnicity and ideology can play within the repertoire of indigenous, ethno-nationalist movements for generating and maintaining social protest. The story of the Mohawk nation's struggle for their aboriginal rights to political sovereignty and economic self-determination, though unfinished, demonstrate that ethno-political and ideological constructs can become dynamic forces for mobilizing group sentiment and protest activity within the highly charged political climate that exists between indigenous, ethno-nationalist groups and the state, particularly when they are combined with an organizational and material resource base. The ability of Mohawk Warrior Movement leaders to resonate their constituents' grievances and interests with their own interests and goals and their success at cultivating and capitalizing on their constituents' sense of responsibility to history and Mohawk nationalism mobilized the kind of sentiment necessary for social movement protest activity during the 1990 Mohawk-Oka conflict.

Although ethno-political and ideological constructs do not necessarily create indigenous ethno-political social movements, they do play an integral role by articulating and elaborating broader movement sentiments others may find appealing. In so doing, they shape the direction of individuals' movement choices. The success of Mohawk Warrior Movement leaders' abilities to garner support and, at times, bridge individuals from seemingly distinct factionalized groups, depended on their ability to frame a compelling ideological ethno-political model. In so doing, they provided the rationale for joining and/or supporting the move- ment and its activities during the 1990 Mohawk-Oka conflict, en- hancing the movement's mobilizing potential then and into the future as well.

Just as the failure of the Meech Lake Accord was a precursor to the 1990 Mohawk-Oka conflict, so too was that conflict a precur- sor to future aboriginal-state legislative relations. In 1991, Canada undertook another attempt at constitutional reform. This time ab- original participation was actively sought by the federal govern- ment. The leaders of the various national aboriginal organizations were asked to formulate their own constitutional reform proposals for incorporation into constitutional negotiations. Several consti- tutional conferences took place during 1992, which resulted in a reform measure, the Charlottetown Accord. This new attempt at constitutional reform incorporated, albeit in modified form, a number of the constitutional positions put forth by aboriginal leaders. The Charlottetown Accord acknowledged that aboriginal peoples have the right to practice their languages, cultures, and traditions and to ensure the integrity of their societies. Further, the Accord stated that aboriginal governments constitute one of three orders of government within Canada. Additionally, the Accord proposed to amend the Canadian Constitution by recog- nizing the inherent right to self-government within Canada for aboriginal peoples. However, the federal government continues to reject any aboriginal claims of sovereignty (the inherent right of aboriginal peoples to exist as separate and autonomous nations).

One might argue that the inclusion of a proposal for some mea- sure of recognition of aboriginal self-determination and govern- ment in the 1992 Charlottestown Constitutional Accord was a direct outgrowth of the 1990 Mohawk-Oka conflict and the ef- forts of Elijah Harper, who impeded the passage of the Meech

Lake Accord. While the Meech Lake Accord was to give certain recognition to Quebec as a distinct society, it was not to do the same for Canada's aboriginal nations. The Charlottestown Constitutional Accord, on the other hand, while not perfect, gave much more recognition to Canada's indigenous population. So, in some ways, while many Mohawks may feel they did not gain anything from the 1990 Mohawk-Oka conflict, this conflict contributed to a larger pressure that motivated Canadian officials to modify its position to include the views of its aboriginal peoples in the new Constitution. This recognition and inclusion constitutes a victory for Mohawks and all other Canadian aboriginal peoples.

Unfortunately, on October 26, 1992, the Charlottetown Accord was rejected by the Canadian electorate. The failure of this attempt at constitutional reform has once again stalemated constitutional recognition of the inherent right of aboriginal self-government, although it will undoubtedly continue to be a dominant position on the political agenda of aboriginal peoples in the future. And so the basis for mobilization and amplification of aboriginal anger via nationhood remains in place, and yet another negotiated (but in this case not enacted) treaty that promised to benefit aboriginal peoples has collapsed. Thus, another historical lesson for aboriginal children and adults was created.

Though (for the time being) the golf course will not expand into "The Pines," it is worth noting that in the aftermath of the 1990 Mohawk-Oka conflict the Canadian federal government has done very little to engage in meaningful discourse concerning negotiations on the larger issues—as they relate to land claims, self-government, and nationhood—that were at the root of (or, reframed) the conflict. To this day, little progress has been made to address the issues of land rights and nationhood which prompted the Mohawk uprising during the spring, summer, and fall of 1990. Further, title to the disputed land that the Canadian federal government had purchased has still not been transferred to the Kanehsatake Mohawks. As such, as of this writing, the Mohawk nation land dispute has yet to be resolved. Kanehsatake Mohawk Negotiating Team member Mavis Etienne explains:

We still don't have title to our territory. The land that was bought, the very piece of land that was at the real heart of the struggle, of what we were here all spring and summer for, is not ours according to their law and their governments. It still belongs to the federal government. And when it is turned over to us, the status of the land will only fall under the use and benefit of the Mohawk people. The government still owns it. Oka doesn't [own it] anymore, but the government does now.

The government still hasn't recognized our historical claim. This is just a polite way of saying you can sit there if you want, but I own that chair. At any time the government can give it back to Oka. We know it; Oka knows it. It's just a 'let them think they can have it' strategy. But only for a while. Then we take it back. They think it buys some time and some peace, that we'll forget, and then it'll be government business all over again. Very little has changed. Quebec and Canada refuse to recognize our sovereignty. The question of jurisdiction over our land as a nation remains unsettled.

Ellen Gabriel, spokesperson for the Kanehsatake Mohawks behind the barricades, explained the lack of progress, in terms of power:

. . . we continue to lack the ability to influence the decision-making process in a systematic way. We need more control over the decision-making process. In that respect, we still don't have the power for that. . . . Power is a difficult question to answer about native people, it's a difficult issue. We feel we have the power over ourselves and the right to exercise that power, but that it is not recognized by the government of Canada. What I'm trying to say is that sovereignty is power, and we consider the Mohawk nation to be a sovereign nation. Therefore, we do have power. But we don't have the ability to recognize or exercise that power until our people become more involved in the government of Canada, in higher positions in the government of Canada. When we have that then we will be able to influence decision making, then we will have power.

So although the Mohawks may have won the battle over the golf course expansion project, they remain a nation at war. Or, to put it in the words of Mohawk Warrior Movement supporter Dale Dion:

> . . . it's not over. It's an ongoing struggle. There are things that remain to be changed, other fights and the same fight to be fought. As long as the issue of land rights remains unresolved, as long as the status of Mohawk nationhood is at issue, the struggle will go on.

This negotiation too has become another historical example for future generations; a new source of responsibility and oppositional ethno-political identity.

Appendix

Persons Interviewed

This list includes all interviewees who allowed their names or quotations to be used. For various reasons, many others requested that their names not appear in the book. The information provided by interviewees who did not want their names used was checked against other sources; information that could not be confirmed elsewhere was eliminated.

Boots, Francis. War chief in the Akwesasne Warrior Longhouse and part of the movement's leadership structure, as well as a member of the Akwesasne Mohawk Negotiating Team.

Bulmer, Mickey "Two Eagles." An Ottawa-Chippewa from Detroit, Michigan, who was part of the broad-based support network.

Bush, Herbert "Big Bear." Member of the Akwesasne Warrior Society.

Catafard, Jean Noel "Christmas." Member of the Kanehsatake Warrior Society.

Cree, John. Kanehsatake Mohawk who took part in the occupation of "The Pines" and a spiritual faith keeper for the Longhouse.

Cross, Ronald "Lasagna." Member of both the Kanehsatake and Kahnawake warrior societies.

David, Joe "Stonecarver." Member of the Kanehsatake Warrior Society.

David, Marie. Kanehsatake Mohawk who took part in the occupation of "The Pines."

David, Valerie. Kanehsatake Mohawk who took part in the occupation of "The Pines."

David Jr., Walter. Kanehsatake Mohawk who took part in the occupation of "The Pines" and a member of the Kanehsatake Mohawk Negotiating Team.

David Sr., Walter. Kanehsatake Mohawk who took part in the occupation of "The Pines" and a member of the Kanehsatake Mohawk Negotiating Team.

David-Cree, Linda. Kanehsatake Mohawk who took part in the occupation of "The Pines."

David-Tolley, Denise. Kanehsatake Mohawk who took part in the occupation of "The Pines" and a member of the Kanehsatake Mohawk Negotiating Team.

Delaronde, Allan. War chief in the Kahnawake Warrior Longhouse and movement leader.

Deom, Joe. Member of the Kahnawake Mohawk Negotiating Team.

Dion, Dale. Member of Mohawk Nation Office; the political voice of the Kahnawake Longhouse and Warrior Society and supporter of the Mohawk Warrior Movement.

Etienne, Debra. Kanehsatake Mohawk who took part in the occupation of "The Pines" and a member of the Kanehsatake legal defense fund-raising group.

Etienne, Mavis. Member of the Kanehsatake Mohawk Negotiating Team.

Gabriel, Allen. Kanehsatake Mohawk who took part in the occupation of "The Pines."

Gabriel, Brenda. Kanehsatake Mohawk who took part in the occupation of "The Pines."

Gabriel, Ellen. Kanehsatake Mohawk who took part in the occupation of "The Pines." Spokesperson for the Mohawks behind the barricades at Kanehsatake and member of the Kanehsatake Mohawk Negotiating Team.

Gabriel, Linda. Kanehsatake Mohawk who took part in the occupation of "The Pines."

Garrow, Minnie "Mama Wolf." Member of the Akwesasne Warrior Society and part of the movement's leadership structure, as well as a member of the Akwesasne Mohawk Negotiating Team.

General, Rowena "Red Deer." Member of the Akwesasne Warrior Society.

Horne, Dean "Sledgehammer." Member of the Kahnawake Warrior Society.

Horne, Randy "Spudwrench." Member of the Kahnawake Warrior Society.

Lazore, Diane. Member of the Akwesasne Warrior Society and Akwesasne Mohawk Negotiating Team.

Lazore, Gordon "Noriega." Member of the Akwesasne Warrior Society.

Maracle, Mark. Member of the Akwesasne Warrior Society.

Martin, Donnie. Assistant war chief in the Kahnawake Warrior Longhouse and part of the movement's leadership structure.

McComber, Mark. Assistant war chief in the Kahnawake Warrior Longhouse and part of the movement's leadership structure.

McComber, Rita. Kahnawake Mohawk elder.

Montour, Mark "Blackjack." Member of both the Akwesasne and Kahnawake warrior societies.

Nelson, Curtis. Kanehsatake Mohawk who took part in the occupation of "The Pines."

Nicholas, Dennis "Psycho." Member of the Kanehsatake Warrior Society.

Oakes, Harold "Beekeeper." Member of the Akwesasne Warrior Society.

Skidders, Robert "Mad Jap." Member of the Akwesasne Warrior Society.

Thomas, Michael. Assistant war chief in the Kahnawake Warrior Longhouse and part of the movement's leadership structure.

Thompson, Loran. Member of the Akwesasne Warrior Society and part of the movement's leadership structure, as well as a member of the Akwesasne Mohawk Negotiating Team.

Tolley, Kelley. Kanehsatake Mohawk who took part in the occupation of "The Pines."

Two Axe, Richard "Boltpin." Member of the Kahnawake Warrior Society.

Wonshon, Nancy. A Chippewa from Detroit, Michigan, who was part of the broad-based support network.

References

Alfred, G. 1995. *Heeding the Voices of our Ancestors*. New York: Oxford University Press.

Akwesasne Notes. 1990. "Taking Over the Nation: Tactics on Terrorism," Early Summer. Rooseveltown, NY.

Ash, R. 1972. *Social Movements in America*. Chicago: Markham.

Benford, R. 1993. "You Could Be the Hundredth Monkey: Collective Action Frames and Vocabularies within the Nuclear Disarmament Movement," *Sociological Quarterly*, 34:195–216.

Boggs, C. 1986. *Social Movements and Political Power*. Philadelphia: Temple University Press.

Bradley, B. 1995. "Building the Santa Fe Greens," *Z Magazine*, June:14–16.

Brand, K. 1990. "Cyclical Aspects of New Social Movements: Waves of Cultural Criticism and Mobilization Cycles on New Middle-Class Radicalism." In R. Dalton and M. Kuechler (eds.), *Challenging the Political Order: New Social and Political Movements in Western Democracies*, New York: Oxford University Press, 23–42.

Campbell, R. 1985. *The People of the Land of the Flint*. Lanham, MD: University Press of America.

Canada, 1878. *Memorandum by J. McGirr, Indian Agent at Oka to Dept. of Interior, March 23.* Ottawa: Dept. of Indian Affairs, Research Branch.

Canada, 1975. *Testimony Before the Joint Committee of the Senate and the House of Commons on Indian Affairs.* Ottawa: Federal Court of Canada.

Canada, 1977. *Testimony Before the Joint Committee of the Senate and the House of Commons on Indian Affairs.* Ottawa: Federal Court of Canada.

Canada, 1991. *The Land Claim Dispute at Oka.* Ottawa: Library of Parliament, Research Branch.

Canada, 1992. *The Amerindians and Inuit in Today's Quebec.* Quebec: Gouvernement du Quebec, Ministry of Indian Affairs.

Chartrand, P. 1992. "The Claims of Aboriginal Peoples in Canada: A Challenge to the Ideas of Confederation in 1867." Paper presented to a conference on Federalism and the Nation State, University of Toronto.

Churchill, W. 1994. *Indians Are Us.* Monroe, ME: Common Courage Press.

Cohen, J. 1985. "Strategy or Identity: New Theoretical Paradigms and Contemporary Social Movements," *Social Research,* 52: 663–716.

Cornell, S. 1988. *The Return of the Native.* New York: Oxford University Press.

Daniels, R. 1980. "The Oka Indians vs. the Seminary of St. Sulpice." In DIAND, *A History of Native Claims Processes in Canada.* Ottawa: Indian and Northern Affairs Canada, Research Branch.

Deloria, V. and Lytle, C. 1984. *The Nations Within.* New York: Pantheon.

DIAND. 1910. *Miscellaneous Correspondence: Oka, 1903–1912.* Ottawa: Canadian Indian Rights Commission Library.

Downey, G. 1986. "Ideology and the Clamshell Identity: Organizational Dilemmas in the Antinuclear Power Movement," *Social Problems,* 33:357–373.

Dwyer, L. 1983. "Structure and Strategy in the Antinuclear Movement." In J. Freeman (ed.), *Social Movements of the Sixties and Seventies*. New York: Longman, 148–161.

Enloe, C. 1981. "The Growth of the State and Ethnic Mobilization," *Ethnic and Racial Studies*, 4:123–136.

Epstein, B. 1990. "Rethinking Social Movement Theory," *Socialist Review*, 20:35–66.

Eyerman, R. and Jamison, A. 1991. *Social Movements: A Cognitive Approach*. University Park, Pennsylvania: The Pennsylvania State University Press.

Fantasia, R. 1988. *Cultures of Solidarity*. Berkeley, California: University of California Press.

Ferree, M. and Hess, B. 1985. *Controversy and Coalition: The New Feminist Movement*. Boston: Twayne.

Ferree, M. and Miller, F. 1985. "Mobilization and Meaning: Some Social Psychological Contributions to the Resource Mobilization Perspective on Social Movements," *Sociological Inquiry*, 55:38–61.

Francis, D. 1983. *A History of the Native Peoples of Quebec, 1760–1867*. Ottawa: Indian and Northern Affairs Canada, Research Branch.

Freeman, J. 1982. *Social Movements of the Sixties and Seventies*. New York: Longman.

Friedman, D. and McAdam, D. 1992. "Collective Identity and Activism: Networks, Choices, and the Life of a Social Movement." In A. Morris and C. Mueller (eds.), *Frontiers in Social Movement Theory*. New Haven: Yale University Press, 156–173.

Gamson, W. 1975. *The Strategy of Social Protest*. Homewood, IL: Dorsey Press.

Gamson, W. 1987. "Introduction." In M. Zald and J. McCarthy (eds.), *Social Movements in an Organizational Society*. New Brunswick: Transaction Books, 1–14.

Gamson, W. 1988. "Political Discourse and Collective Action." In B. Klandermans, H. Kriesi, and S. Tarrow (eds.), *From Struc-*

ture to Action: Comparing Social Movement Research Across Cultures. Greenwich, CT: JAI Press.

Gerlach, L. 1983. "Movements of Revolutionary Change: Some Structural Characteristics." In J. Freeman (ed.), *Social Movements of the Sixties and Seventies*, New York: Longman, 133–147.

Gerlach, L. and Hine, V. 1970. *People, Power, Change: Movements of Social Transformation*. Indianapolis: Bobbs-Merrill.

Getty, I. and Lussier, A. 1983. *As Long As the Sun Shines and the Water Flows: A Reader in Canadian Native Studies*. Vancouver: Nakoda Institute, University of British Columbia.

Globe and Mail. 1990. "One Little Indian," September, 25. Toronto, Canada.

Grimes, B. 1988. *Ethnologue: Languages of the World*. Dallas: Summer Institute of Linguistics.

Gurr, T. 1993. *Minorities at Risk: A Global View of Ethnopolitical Conflicts*. Washington, DC: United States Institute of Peace Press.

Hall, L. 1987. *Gayanerakowa. The Constitution of the Iroquois Confederacy*. Self-published mimeo.

Hornung, R. 1991. *One Nation Under the Gun*. Toronto: Stoddart Publishing.

Horowitz, I. 1985. *Ethnic Groups in Conflict*. Berkeley: University of California Press.

Hunt, S. and Benford, R. 1993. "Identity Talk in the Peace and Justice Movement," *Journal of Contemporary Ethnography*, 22:488–517.

Hutchins, P. 1977. *The Oka Indians Land Claim*. Ottawa: Indian and Northern Affairs Canada, Research Branch.

Iroquois Grand Council. 1989. "Position Statement," December, 23. Onondaga, NY.

Jenkins, C, 1983. "Resource Mobilization Theory and the Study of Social Movements," *Annual Review of Sociology*, 9:527–553.

Jenson, J. 1995. "What's in a Name: Nationalist Movements and Public Discourse." In H. Johnston and B. Klandermans (eds.), *Social Movements and Culture*, Minneapolis, MN: University of Minnesota Press, 107–126.

Jhappan, R. 1993. "Inherency, Three Nations and Collective Rights: The Evolution of Aboriginal Constitutional Discourse from 1982 to the Charlottetown Accord," *International Journal of Canadian Studies*, no. 7–8, (Spring-Fall).

Johansen, B. 1993. *Life and Death in Mohawk Country*. Golden, CO: North American Press.

Johnston, H. and Klandermans, B. 1995. "The Cultural Analysis of Social Movements." In H. Johnston and B. Klandermans (eds.), *Social Movements and Culture*, Minneapolis, MN: University of Minnesota Press, 3–24.

Kanehsatake Negotiating Team. 1990. "Communique," August, 21.

Klandermans, B. 1984. "Mobilization and Participation: Social Psychological Expansions of Resource Mobilization Theory," *American Sociological Review*, 49:583–600.

Klandermans, B. 1986. "New Social Movements and Resource Mobilization: The European and the American Approach," *Internation Journal of Mass Emergencies and Disasters*, 4:13–37.

Klandermans, B. 1989. "Introduction: Social Movement Organizations and the Study of Social Movements." In B. Klandermans (ed.), *Organizing for Change: Social Movement Organizations in Europe and the United States*, Vol.2. Greenwich, CT: JAI Press, 1–17.

Klandermans, B. 1992. "The Social Construction of Protest and Multiorganizational Fields." In A. Morris and C. Mueller (eds.), *Frontiers in Social Movements Theory*, New Haven, CT: Yale University Press.

Klandermans, B. 1994. "Transient Identities?: Membership Patterns in the Dutch Peace Movement." In E. Larana, H. Johnston, and J. Gusfield (ed.), *New Social Movements: From Ideology to Identity*, Philadelphia, PA: Temple University Press, 168–184.

Klandermans, B. and Oegema, D. 1987. "Potentials, Networks, Motivations, and Barriers: Steps Toward Participation in Social Movements," *American Sociological Review*, 52:519–531.

Klandermans, B. and Tarrow, S. 1988. "Mobilization into Social Movements: Synthesizing European and American Approaches," *From Structure to Action: Comparing Movement Participation Across Cultures*, Vol. 1. Greenwich, CT: JAI Press, 1–38.

Lacan, J. 1876. *A Historical Notice on the Difficulties Arisen Between the Seminary of St. Sulpice of Montreal and Certain Indians at Oka, Lake of Two Mountains: A Mere Case of Property Rights.* Ottawa: Canadian Indian Rights Commission Library.

Lacoste, A. 1880. *The Seminary of Montreal: Their Rights and Titles.* Ottawa: Canadian Indian Rights Commission Library.

Landsman, G. 1988. *Sovereignty and Symbol.* Albuquerque: University of New Mexico Press.

Levinson, D. 1993. *Encyclopedia of World Cultures*, Vols. I–IV. Boston: Kittall.

Liebich, A. 1983. "Straussianism and Ideology." In A. Parel (ed.), *Ideology, Philosophy and Politics.* Waterloo: Wilfrid Laurier University Press.

Long, D. 1992. "Culture, Ideology, and Militancy: The Movement of Native Indians in Canada, 1969–1991." In W.E. Carroll (ed.), *Organising Dissent: Contemporary Social Movements in Theory and Practice*, Toronto: Garamond.

Malone Evening Telegram, 1968. "Mohawks Seize Bridge," April 3. New York: Malone.

Malone Evening Telegram, 1970. "Mohawks Occupy Islands," May 15. New York: Malone.

Malone Evening Telegram, 1989. "Troopers Hall Off Slot Machines," June 1. New York: Malone.

Matthiessen, P. 1991. *In the Spirit of Crazy Horse*, New York: Viking.

McAdam, D. 1982. *Political Process and the Development of Black Insurgency, 1930–1970.* Chicago: University of Chicago Press.

McAdam, D. 1988. *Freedom Summer.* New York: Oxford University Press.

McAdam, D. 1994. "Culture and Social Movements." In E. Larana, H. Johnston, and J. Gusfield (eds.), *New Social Movements: From Ideology to Identity*, Philadephia, PA: Temple University Press, 36–57.

McAdam, D., McCarthy, J. and Zald, M. 1988. "Social Movements." In N. Smelser (ed.), *Handbook of Sociology*. Newbury Park, CA: Sage Publications, 695–737.

McCarthy, J. and Zald, M. 1973. *The Trend of Social Movements in America: Professionalization and Resource Mobilization*. Morristown, NJ: General Learning Press.

McCarthy, J. and Zald, M. 1977. "Resource Mobilization and Social Movements: A Partial Theory," *American Journal of Sociology*, 82:1212–1241.

Melucci, A. 1985. "The Symbolic Challenge of Contemporary Movements," *Social Research*, 52:781–816.

Melucci, A. 1988a. "Getting Involved: Identity and Mobilization in Social Movements," *From Structure to Action: Comparing Movement Participation Across Cultures*, Vol. 1. Greenwich, CT: JAI Press, 329–348.

Melucci, A. 1988b. "Social Movements and the Democratization of Everyday Life." In J. Keane (ed.), *Civil Society and the State*. London: Verso, 245–260.

Melucci, A. 1989. *Nomads of the Present: Social Movements and Individual Needs in Contemporary Society*. Philadelphia: Temple University Press.

Melucci, A. 1994. "A Strange Kind of Newness: What's New in New Social Movements." In E. Larana, H. Johnston, and J. Gusfield (eds.), *New Social Movements: From Ideology to Identity*, Philadephia, PA: Temple University Press, 101–130.

Miller, J. R. 1991. *Skyscrapers Hide the Heavens*. Toronto, Canada: University of Toronto Press.

Modavi, N. 1992. "The Political Economy of State Intervention in Grass-roots Mobilization: A Case Study of Community Opposition to Golf Course Development in Hawaii." Paper presented at the annual meeting of the American Sociological Association, Pittsburgh, PA.

Mohawk Nation Council. 1989. Press release, July, 24.

Mohawk Women of Kahnawake. 1990. Press release, August, 31.

Montreal Gazette, 1973a. "Mohawks Begin Evictions," September 5. Montreal, Canada.

Montreal Gazette, 1973b. "Mohawks Force White Residents Off Reserve," October 15. Montreal, Canada.

Montreal Gazette, 1988. "RCMP's Raid Mohawks," June 10. Montreal, Canada.

Montreal Gazette, 1989a. "Oka Golf Club Announces Expansion," March 4. Montreal, Canada.

Montreal Gazette, 1989b. "Mohawks Protest Golf Course Expansion," April 3. Montreal, Canada.

Montreal Gazette, 1989c. "Golf Course Tree Cutting Ceremony Halted," August 1. Montreal, Canada.

Montreal Gazette, 1989d. "Golf Course Moratorium," August 5. Montreal, Canada.

Montreal Gazette, 1990a. "Board of Directors Approve Golf Course Expansion," March 10. Montreal, Canada.

Montreal Gazette, 1990b. "Mohawks Block Pines," March 11. Montreal, Canada.

Montreal Gazette, 1990c. "Oka Hires Contractors Then Cancels," May 1. Montreal, Canada.

Montreal Gazette, 1990d. "Mohawks Agree to Negotiate," May 2. Montreal, Canada.

Montreal Gazette, 1990e. "Quebec Rules Mohawks Must Remove Barricades," June 30. Montreal, Canada.

Montreal Gazette, 1990f. "Confrontation with Mohawks," July 11. Montreal, Canada.

Montreal Gazette, 1990g. "Defiant Mohawks," July 12. Montreal, Canada.

Montreal Gazette, 1990h. "Mohawks Engage in Informal Talks with Government," July 13. Montreal, Canada.

Montreal Gazette, 1990i. "Mohawks Reach Agreement," July 15. Montreal, Canada.

Montreal Gazette, 1990j. "Mohawks Declare Agreement Void," July 16. Montreal, Canada.

Montreal Gazette, 1990k. "Deal in the Works," July 26. Montreal, Canada.

Montreal Gazette, 1990l. "Mohawks Given 48 Hours," August 5. Montreal, Canada.

Montreal Gazette, 1990m. "Defense Act Invoked," August 8. Montreal, Canada.

Montreal Gazette, 1990n. "Formal Negotiations with Mohawks Begin," August 16. Montreal, Canada.

Montreal Gazette, 1990o. "Armed Forces Replace SQ at Barricades," August 20. Montreal, Canada.

Montreal Gazette, 1990p. "Mohawk Negotiations Resume," August 24. Montreal, Canada.

Montreal Gazette, 1990q. "Federal Tropps to Remove Barricades," August 27. Montreal, Canada.

Montreal Gazette, 1990r. "Mohawks Help Dismantle Barricades," August 29. Montreal, Canada.

Montreal Gazette, 1990s. "Army Ends Standoff at Kahnawake," September 1. Montreal, Canada.

Montreal Gazette, 1990t. "Kanehsatake Under Military Occupation," September 3. Montreal, Canada.

Montreal Gazette, 1990u. "Last Mohawk Holdouts Emerge," September 26. Montreal, Canada.

Morris, A. 1984. *The Origins of the Civil Rights Movement: Black Communities Organizing for Change*. New York: Free Press.

Morris, A. and Mueller, C. 1992. *Frontiers in Social Movement Theory*. New Haven, CT: Yale University Press.

Morrison, R. and Wilson, C. 1991. *Native Peoples: The Canadian Experience*. Toronto: McClelland & Stewart.

Mueller, C. 1987. "Collective Consciousness, Identity Transformation, and the Rise of Women in Public Office in the United States." In M. Fainsod-Katzenstein and C. McClung-Meuller (eds.), *The Women's Movements of the United States and Western Europe: Consciousness, Political Opportunity, and Public Policy*. Philadelphia: Temple University Press, 89–108.

Nagel, J. 1980. "The Conditions of Ethnic Separatism: The Kurds in Turkey, Iran, and Iraq," *Ethnicity*, 7:279–97.

Nagel, J. 1981. "Politics and the Organization of Collective Action," *Political Behavior*, 3:87–116.

Nagel, J. 1982. "The Political Mobilization of Native Americans," *The Social Science Journal*, 19:37–45.

Nagel, J. 1986. "The Political Construction of Ethnicity." In S. Olzak & J. Nagel (eds.), *Competitive Ethnic Relations*. New York: Academic Press, 93–114.

Nagel, J. 1988. "The Roots of Red Power: Demographic and Organizational Bases of American Indian Activism, 1950–1980." Paper presented at the Annual Meetings of the American Sociological Association, Chicago, IL.

Nagel, J. 1989. "American Indian Repertoires of Contention." Paper presented at the annual meeting of the American Sociological Association, San Francisco, CA.

Nagel, J. 1992. "Constructing Ethnicity: Creating and Recreating Ethnic Identity and Culture." Paper presented at the annual meeting of the American Sociological Association, Pittsburgh, PA.

Nagel, J. 1996. *American Indian Ethnic Renewal*. New York: Oxford University Press.

Nagel, J. and Snipp, M. 1991. "Ethnic Reorganization: American Indian Strategies for Survival." Paper presented at the annual meeting of the American Sociological Association, Cincinnati, OH.

National Public Radio. 1995. "All Things Considered." August 17.

Nietschmann, B. 1987. "Militarization and Indigenous Peoples: The Third World War," *Cultural Survival Quarterly*, 11:1–16.

Oberschall, A. 1973. *Social Conflict and Social Movements*. Englewood Cliffs, NJ: Prentice-Hall.

Oka Municipal Council, 1989. Council Meeting Minutes, March 3. Oka, Quebec, Canada.

Oka Municipal Council, 1990a. Council Meeting Minutes, March 5. Oka, Quebec, Canada.

Oka Municipal Council, 1990b. Council Meeting Minutes, May 8. Oka, Quebec, Canada.

Oka Municipal Council, 1990c. Council Meeting Minutes, July 26. Oka, Quebec, Canada.

Oka Municipal Council, 1990d. Council Meeting Minutes, August 9. Oka, Quebec, Canada.

Olzak, S. 1982. "Ethnic Mobilization in Quebec," *Ethnic and Race Studies*, 5:253–275.

Olzak, S. 1983. "Contemporary Ethnic Mobilization," *Annual Review of Sociology*, 9:355–374.

Ornstein, T. 1973. *The First Peoples in Quebec*. Montreal: Thunderbird Press.

Ottawa, House of Commons. 1991. "Minutes of Proceedings and Evidence of the Standing Committee on Aboriginal Affairs," March 12.

Pariseau, C. 1974. *Les Troubles de 1860–1880 a Oka: Choc de deux Cultures*. Masters thesis. Montreal: McGill University.

Parker, A. 1916. *The Great Law of Peace*. Ottawa: Canadian National Archives.

Pena, M. 1995. *Theologies and Liberation in Peru: The Role of Ideas in Social Movements*. Philadelphia, PA: Temple University Press.

Press Republican. 1990. "Mohawks Opposed to Gambling," May 12. Plattsburgh, NY.

Quebec Superior Court. 1910. *Angus Corinthe, Plaintiff vs. the Ecclesiastics of the Seminary of St. Sulpice of Montreal, Defendants*. Ottawa: Canadian Indian Rights Commission Library.

Quebec Superior Court, 1990a. *Oka Municipal Council, Plaintiff vs. Mohawks, Defendant*, April 26. Ottawa: Canadian Indian Rights Commission Library.

Quebec Superior Court, 1990b. *Oka Municipal Council, Plaintiff vs. Mohawks, Defendants*, June 7. Ottawa: Canadian Indian Rights Commission Library.

Quebec Superior Court, 1990c. *Oka Municipal Council, Plaintiff vs. Mohawks, Defendants*, June 30. Ottawa: Canadian Indian Rights Commission Library.

Rochon, M. 1991. *Oka—Kanehsatake—Summer 1990: A Collective Shock*. Report of the Commission des droits de la personne du Quebec, April.

Scott, A. 1990. *Ideology and the New Social Movements*. London: Unwin Hyman.

Smith, A. 1981. *The Ethnic Revival*. Cambridge: Cambridge University Press.

Snow, D. and Benford, R. 1988. "Ideology, Frame Resonance and Participant Mobilization," *International Social Movement Research*, 1:197–217.

Snow, D., Rochford, E., Worden, S. and Benford, R. 1986. "Frame Alignment Processes, Micromobilization, and Movement Participation," *American Sociological Review*, 51:464–481.

Snow, D., Zurcher, L. and Ekland-Olson, S. 1980. "Social Networks and Social Movements: A Microstructural Approach to Differential Recruitment," *American Sociological Review*, 45:787–801.

Swindler, A. 1995. "Cultural Power and Social Movements." In H. Johnston and B. Klandermans (eds.), *Social Movements and Culture*, Minneapolis, MN: University of Minnesota Press, 25–40.

Syracuse Post Standard, 1971a. "Mohawks Halt Construction," July 15. Syracuse, NY.

Syracuse Post Standard, 1971b. "Mohawks Engage in Confrontation," August 1. Syracuse, NY.

Syracuse Post Standard. 1990. "Oka Holdouts Arrested," September, 28. Syracuse, NY.

Tarrow, S. 1988. "National Politics and Collective Action: Recent Theory and Research in Western Europe and the United States," *Annual Review of Sociology*, 14:421–40.

Taylor, V. 1989. "Social Movement Continuity: The Women's Movement in Abeyance," *American Sociological Review*, 54:761–775.

Taylor, V. and Whittier, N. 1992. "Collective Identity in Social Movement Communities: Lesbian Feminist Mobilization." In A. Morris & C. Mueller (eds.), *Frontiers in Social Movement Theory*. New Haven: Yale University Press, 104–129.

Tilly, C. 1978. *From Mobilization to Revolution*. Reading, MA: Addison-Wesley.

Tilly, C. and Shorter, E. 1974. *Strikes in France, 1830–1968*. New York: Cambridge University Press.

Touraine, A. 1985. "An Introduction to the Study of Social Movements," *Social Research*, 52:749–787.

Trigger, B. 1977. *The Indians and the Age of New France*. Ottawa: Canadian Historical Association.

Trotsky, L. 1965. *The Permanent Revolution*. New York: Pioneer Press.

Tucker, K. 1989. "Ideology and Social Movements: The Contributions of Habermas," *Sociological Inquiry*, 59:30–47.

Van den Berghe, P. 1983. "Class, Race, and Ethnicity in Africa," *Ethnic and Racial Studies*, 6:221–36.

Villeneuve, L. and Francis, D. 1984. "The Oka Indians." In DIAND, *The Historical Background of Indian Reserves and Settlements in the Province of Quebec*. Ottawa: Indian and Northern Affairs Canada, Research Branch.

Webster's New World Dictionary. 1986. New York: Prentice-Hall Press.

Whittier, N. and Taylor, V. 1989. "The Construction of a Politicized Collective Identity: Culture, Identity, and Symbolism in Lesbian Feminist Communities." Paper presented at the annual meetings of the American Sociological Association, San Francisco, CA.

Whittier, N. and Taylor, V. 1991. "Collective Identity and Feminist Activism: Lesbian Feminism and the Survival of the Women's Movement." Paper presented at the annual meetings of the American Sociological Association, Cincinnati, OH.

Williams, R. 1994. "The Sociology of Ethnic Conflicts: Comparative International Perspectives," *Annual Review of Sociology*, 20:49–79.

Women of Kahnawake. 1990. "Open Letter to the Community," August 23.

Yinger, J. M. 1985. "Ethnicity," *Annual Review of Sociology*, 11:151–80.

Yinger, J. M. 1986. "Intersecting Strands in the Theorizing of Race and Ethnic Relations." In J. Rex and D. Mason (eds.), *Theories of Race and Ethnic Relations*. Cambridge: Cambridge University Press, 20–41.

York, G. and Pindera, L. 1991. *People of the Pines*. Toronto: Little, Brown & Company.

Zald, M. and McCarthy, J. 1979. *The Dynamics of Social Movements*. Mass.: Winthrop Publishers.

Index

Printed in the United States
20706LVS00006B/340-345

9 780791 432129